UNRAVELING THE FAMILY SECRET

JUBILEE HADDESSA

Copyright 2024 by Jubilee Haddessa

All rights reserved, including the right to reproduce this book or portions thereof in any form whatsoever or by any means. No part of this book may be reproduced, stored in a retrieval system, or transmitted by any means without written permission of the author, except as provided by United States of America copyright law.

First edition: December 2024

Book cover and design by
Book Puma Author Services
BookPumaEdit.com

ISBN: 979-8-218-51910-0

To my late father, who always believed in me, no matter what.

Introduction

This story chronicles the journey to find my biological second-great-grandfather on my father's side, Charles F. Rose, and his relationship with my second-great-grandmother, Sarah Tonge. This quest sustained me through the COVID-19 pandemic; it saved my life and continues to do so to this day.

In the words of a popular television character: "Once a wise man told me, 'Family doesn't end in blood.' But it doesn't start there either. Family cares about you. Not what you can do for them. Family is there for the good, bad, all of it. They got your back, even when it hurts. That's family."[1]

This quote has caused me to reflect often on James Sabey and what he did for Sarah Tonge and her children. He loved them as his own, taking them in when he did not have to.

It also made me think about family secrets, scandals, embarrassment, and having an affinity for someone long-dead when you don't really have that relationship with the living. Or, easily having an affinity for someone you just met, but having it for your own immediate family feels like pulling teeth. It makes me think about how a person can still have an effect on his or her descendants more than 130 years later. Their stories might even save their descendants' lives from beyond the grave.

Digging into history found the truth in a father-daughter relationship when most believed the nasty gossip. Digging into history found a long-lost biological second-great-grandfather, originally lost to time because his daughter was conceived in prison. One little rumor—incest—turned several generations against a man they had no right to judge. His descendants didn't look into it. No one talked about it. It was taboo.

The division in the family line was like the Hatfields and the McCoys; that family feud has been going on for several generations. These two families started fighting and made history while doing so, yet no one alive today can truly say how that feud started.

People heard the word "incest" and stopped researching right there. They turned their backs on that family line for generations because they couldn't be bothered to investigate further and discover the truth. They couldn't be bothered to find out that the incest story was a pack of wild lies. Just rumors! But even if it wasn't a lie, the allegations and court proceedings happened more than a hundred years ago. It's history at this point. And history is full of weird, depraved, and sickening stories that people are fascinated by and cannot get enough of.

Have you ever heard a family rumor about a great-grandparent or a second-great-grandparent? Have you heard a rumor that stopped you in your tracks? Or, have you ever had a parent drop a bombshell in your lap that changes what you thought you knew your entire life?

Earth-shattering revelations by family members about family members are always hard to take. Rumors destroy lives, whether they were started today or a hundred years ago. They are cruel, and some must be researched before the truth is found out. Sometimes, you need to take a stand against family members and dig deeper into the rumors to right the wrongs of history. It only takes one person to stand up and ask more questions. The truth will always find a way to the surface.

There will always be those who will not want to know the facts, but finding the truth will

---

1 CW (TV Series), "Supernatural," Season 10, Episode 17, *Inside Man*, Quote said by Dean Winchester to Crowley.

be worth it in the end if even one person listens to the family detective. That is what I call myself: The family detective, the protector of the flame (stories). I am the one who wants the truth to be known, no matter where it might lead. Family history is my passion, and I am doing all I can to keep the memory of the ones who came before me alive.

We need to acknowledge that people in the past were only human, too. We need to learn from them, honor them, and talk about them, no matter what happened to them or what they did.

Different people in my family knew bits and pieces of this story over the years, although the accounts varied wildly. It was almost like the game of Telephone, where everything gets so twisted around from the original as it passes from person to person.

I had asked one person in particular my question about my great-grandmother's surname being Rose on the 1900 United States census. That person got mad at me and said, "James Sabey is Maude's father. Leave it alone."[2] That is all well and good, but we are still responsible for finding and learning about the Rose line. That encounter also told me two very important things. First, there was indeed a juicy story or two to be told. Second, this cousin did not truly know me at all. I would figure it out myself . . . eventually. It did not matter how long it took.

It was never my intention to disregard James Sabey as the man who took Maude in as his own daughter. I just wanted to know about the Rose line. It was my intention to find the lost, to give them the chance to come to light again. To be known and to have their names cleared of any wrongdoing. To fix the wrongs in history so we do not run headlong into the darkness and repeat the past. To give them a voice from the dust. Knowledge is power, and if we do not learn from our past, especially our own family's past, we may be destined to repeat it.

Research is also fun. You never know what unexpected discoveries you will make, such as one side of the family throwing the other side in jail.

One person gave me a little bit of information about Charles Rose when I asked her about him: "He was a redhead jailer. No one even knew his name . . . only that he and Sarah Tonge conceived Maude in prison."

Another person was playful when I told him that I had found Charles Rose: "You mean that red headed cowboy from Wyoming? I knew I couldn't be the only black sheep of the family."

Telephone, I tell you. Over the years, the truth has been changed—twisted even—and now no one really knows the truth. Or, at least, not yet.

---

2 FamilySearch, "United States Census, 1900," database with images, FamilySearch, (https://www.familysearch.org: accessed 22 Aug 2010), Maud Alice Rose in household of Sarah Sabey, Charleston, Wallsburg, Center, Daniels Precincts Charleston town, Wasatch, Utah, United States; citing enumeration district (ED) 170, sheet 13A, family 194, NARA microfilm publication T623 (Washington, D.C.: National Archives and Records Administration, 1972.); FHL microfilm 1,241,688.

1 Discovering the Family Secret

The quest of a lifetime started a little over a decade ago. My mother dropped a bombshell on the way home from the last Haddessa-Sabey reunion. The reunions ended because my grandfather and all of his siblings had passed, and no one else wanted to do the work to keep the tradition going.

"You know, you aren't actually related to the Sabeys," my mother said nonchalantly from the passenger seat.

For a moment, I wasn't sure I heard her right. I had to pull over. "What?! Explain!"

It felt like my world was shaken and shattered. For twenty-five years of my life, every summer included the Haddessa-Sabey reunion. That reunion started with my father's paternal grandparents, John Haddessa and Maude Sabey.

"Your great-grandmother Maude's surname on the 1900 United States federal census is not Sabey," my mother continued. "Actually, it's Rose."

"You'll have to show me when we get home." I was in shock. My reality had been turned upside-down, and I had no idea how to handle it.

When we arrived home, we didn't even unload the car. My mother and I went straight to her home office, which was previously my younger brother's bedroom. This room is so small that a queen bed will swallow the room and only leave maybe a foot on three sides of the bed to move around. Before it was my mom's home office, it was my brother and I's shared bedroom until I was about eight years old. We slept in twin bunk beds in that room.

This bedroom also had a walk-in closet—about four feet wide and six feet deep—where my mother set up her desk. She sat down and booted up her desktop computer. As my mom logged in to FamilySearch, I retrieved one of the kitchen chairs from the dining room table to sit next to her.

Mom pulled up that 1900 census for Wasatch County, Utah, and showed me the Sabey household.[3] For a few moments, I could not believe what I read. It took a minute for what I was seeing to dawn on me and for a light bulb to go off in my head.

Transcript:

Name: James Sabey
Sex: Male
Age: 66
Birth Date: May 1834
Birthplace: England
Arrival Date: 1865
Marital Status: Married
Race: White
Years Married: 3
Relationship to Head of Household: Head
Father's Birthplace: England
Mother's Birthplace: England
Event Date: 1900
Event Place: Charleston, Wasatch, Utah, United States
Line Number: 1
Sheet Letter: A
Sheet Number: 13
Affiliate Publication Number: T623
Affiliate Name: The U.S. National Archives and Records Administration (NARA)

Name: Sarah Sabey
Sex: Female
Age: 36
Birth Date: Sep 1864
Birthplace: England
Arrival Date: 1873
Marital Status: Married
Race: White
Number of Living Children: 4
Years Married: 3
Number of Children: 4
Relationship to Head of Household: Wife
Father's Birthplace: England
Mother's Birthplace: England
Event Date: 1900
Event Place: Charleston, Wasatch, Utah, United States
Household Identifier: 194
Line Number: 4
Sheet Letter: A
Sheet Number: 13
Affiliate Publication Number: T623
Affiliate Name: The U.S. National Archives and Records Administration (NARA)

Name: Maud Alice Rose (My family has always spelled Maude with an E. It is misspelled on this document).
Relationship to Head: Stepdaughter
Sex: F
Age: 11

---

3 "United States Census, 1900," database with images, *FamilySearch*, (https://www.familysearch.org: accessed 22 Aug 2010), Maud Alice Rose in household of Sarah Sabey, Charleston, Wallsburg, Center, Daniels Precincts Charleston town, Wasatch, Utah, United States; citing enumeration district (ED) 170, sheet 13A, family 194, NARA microfilm publication T623 (Washington, D.C.: National Archives and Records Administration, 1972.); FHL microfilm 1,241,688.

Birthplace: Wyoming

Name: Roy Rose
Relationship to Head: Stepson
Sex: M
Age: 8
Birthplace: Utah

Name: Jay Spradley (On this document, Spratley is spelled with a D instead of a T. Most other documents spell it with a T.)
Relationship to Head: Stepson
Sex: M
Age: 4
Birthplace: Utah

Name: Lacy Sabey
Relationship to Head: Daughter
Sex: F
Age: 1
Birthplace: Utah

Well, I'll be! Sure enough, Maude's surname was Rose, not Sabey. This was the document that launched my ten-year investigation. For ten years, all I knew about my biological second-great-grandfather was that his surname was Rose and that he was from Germany. He also had to have connections to Evanston, Uinta County, Wyoming, because that was the birthplace of Maude on December 8, 1888.

The 1900 census also shows new information about Maude's two younger brothers.[4] Roy's surname was also Rose, and his father was from Germany. This means that Maude and Roy may have had the same father. Jay's surname was Spratley, and his father was from Utah. That meant he had a different father than Maude and Roy.

There was another family line to find. No one ever talked about the Spratleys, either. These were two family lines that no one to my knowledge was even looking at. Two family lines needed to be found and to be researched. Challenge accepted!

On and off for ten years, I looked into these two family lines. Along the way, there was one roadblock after another:
- Evanston, Wyoming, had fires that destroyed a lot of their records.
- My dad's cousins would always shut me down when I asked about the Roses and Spratleys.
- My dad was not a lot of help because he was diagnosed with dementia fourteen years ago. He passed away in late August 2022.
- "James Sabey is Maude's father. Leave it alone." Enough said.

We need to understand who our ancestors were to fully understand ourselves. Their trials of faith and how they lived can have a healing effect on our very souls. These stories are in the very fabric of my life, resonating deep in my bones. Piecing these stories back together one shattered piece at a time has created something beautiful in my soul. The Rose line and the Spratley line seemed to have been cast aside, and they needed to be found.

In 2019, I finally broke through one of the proverbial brick walls standing in the way of my family history, only to reveal several more behind it. It was almost like the more information I gathered, the more questions I had.

The Ancestry.com DNA test I took in 2016 has given me a lot of information, such as my ethnicity and identifying some of my living relatives. The DNA itself does not change, but the DNA testing company's science does. That meant that more information would come in time or would change.

In April 2019, I sent email requests to the Utah State Archives in Salt Lake City, Utah, for Roy Rose's and Jay Spratley's birth certificates. No luck.

Utah did not legally require government agencies to keep birth records until 1898.[5]

Wyoming didn't require birth records to be kept

---

4 FamilySearch, "United States Census, 1900," database with images, *FamilySearch*, (https://www.familysearch.org: accessed 22 Aug 2010), Maud Alice Rose in household of Sarah Sabey, Charleston, Wallsburg, Center, Daniels Precincts Charleston town, Wasatch, Utah, United States; citing enumeration district (ED) 170, sheet 13A, family 194, NARA microfilm publication T623 (Washington, D.C.: National Archives and Records Administration, 1972.); FHL microfilm 1,241,688.

5 Utah State Archives, "The Birth Certificate of Roy Rose Sabey and Jay Spratley Sabey," Utah State Archives, Salt Lake City, Utah, (Utah State Archives: Accessed 13 Apr 2019.) Negative Results.

until 1909.[6] Maude's birth certificate was not found anywhere I searched. It might not even exist. That was another dead end.

The more extended family members I asked about these lines, the dodgier they became and the more I wanted to know. I knew there was a story there. All stories want to be told, no matter what they have to reveal. There is something within the human soul that craves stories.

This story wanted to be told and would not let me give up my pursuit of the truth. The discovery that Maude, Roy, and Jay might not have birth records did not deter me. It only made me more determined to find out anything I could about them. I am a firm believer in finding every document I can about my ancestors because every document adds to a person's story—the good, the bad, and the tragic.

There is something you need to know about me: The more someone tells me I can't or shouldn't do something without giving me a very good reason as to why, the more I want to do the exact opposite of what they are telling me to do. This stubbornness and natural curiosity will get me into trouble sometimes. It has also turned me into a determined learner and researcher on any number of subjects.

The more I learned how records were kept in the United States in the 1800s, the more records I found to search. That forced me to think outside the box, to become a more rounded person, and to become a better investigator. I am constantly learning about new ways to do research. New leads are always popping up—and in surprising ways—just by living my life. My sister calls me the family detective. She always asks me how the sleuthing is going.

---

6 Uinta County Records, Evanston, Wyoming, "The Birth Record of Maude Rose Tonge Sabey (1889)," Uinta County Records, Evanston, Wyoming, (http://www.uintacounty.com: accessed 13 August 2005,) Negative Results.

2 The Sleuthing Is Never Over

On a Saturday in May 2019, I decided to take my mom with me to Salt Lake City, Utah, to visit the Family History Center of The Church of Jesus Christ of Latter-Day Saints on Temple Square. Armed only with determination, the 1900 census, and a prayer of knowing that was where I needed to be that day, I hoped to get some help with finding anything about Mr. Rose or Mr. Spratley.[7]

The FamilySearch Family History Library in Salt Lake—I know this is a mouthful, but that is the library's name—is the largest family history/genealogy library in the world. It has five levels. The main floor hosts meet-and-greets with missionaries from the Church of Jesus Christ of Latter-day Saints who are ready to help direct you to the correct floor for your search. This floor also has large kiosks playing videos about family history, computer stations, and large pictures of pedigree charts and fan charts. There is also a good-sized break room. Patrons can bring their own lunches from home or buy full meals from the vending machines.

The second floor houses the records of the United States and Canada. We were directed there, but we had no idea where to start. Thousands of microfilms lived in floor-to-ceiling filing cabinets, and many books filled shelves. Microfilm readers—the older kind of machine that makes a whirling sound when you roll through a microfilm quickly and the new ones that give you a digital picture of the film when you run the film through it—were available for use.

When I was about eight years old, my parents started to take me with them any time they wanted to go the Family History Library. My parents would sit me down at one of the older-style microfilm readers.[8] It was about four feet tall and had a shelf near the top where you would thread a microfilm from one reel onto a second reel and through the projector. A bright light projected the image onto a slightly slanted white surface on the bottom of the machine, where you could read the negative.[9] The hand crank on the right side of the machine was used to roll the film forward or backward, fast or slow. A person could also take a picture with the machine and have the information printed off on a copier.

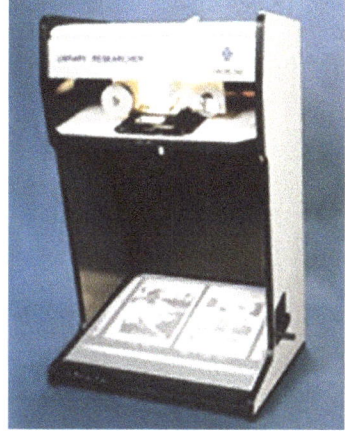
An old microfilm reader

Microfilm, a roll of negative pictures

They would give me a stack of microfilms to look at and a piece of paper with an ancestor's name on it. They would then proceed to tell me that I wasn't to come find them until I found that ancestor's name on a microfilm document. It became a game to me, and I

---

7 FamilySearch, "United States Census, 1900," database with images, *FamilySearch*, (https://www.familysearch.org: accessed 22 Aug 2010), Maud Alice Rose in household of Sarah Sabey, Charleston, Wallsburg, Center, Daniels Precincts Charleston town, Wasatch, Utah, United States; citing enumeration district (ED) 170, sheet 13A, family 194, NARA microfilm publication T623 (Washington, D.C.: National Archives and Records Administration, 1972.); FHL microfilm 1,241,688

8 A3Genealogy, historical and genealogy research specialists, Kathleen Brandt, Sunday, February 7, 2010, image of a microfilm reader, (https://blog.a3genealogy.com/2010/02/sentimental-sunday-microfilm-readers.html?showComment=1266153109648&m=0 : Accessed 16 March 2024).

9 Picture of Microfilm. Image Online, (https://bmiimaging.com/wp-content/uploads/2014/06/304.jpg Accessed: 30 March 2024.)

still remember the whirling of the reader as I used the hand crank to move the film through the projector. Rewinding the films made a higher-pitched whirling sound. The faster I could spin the hand crank, the higher-pitched the whirling would become. I did find some of the names my parents asked me to locate. I do not remember what any of those names were now, but this was what started my passion for family history. This was an immersive and tactile experience in research.

There were also many computers on the second floor that patrons could utilize. My mom and I knew we needed professional help. There were many missionaries for the Church of Jesus Christ of Latter-Day Saints there, and we asked the first sister missionary that we saw to help us.

She sat down with us at a computer and started searching. After about an hour or two on Mr. Rose, she stated, "I wish I knew his given name."

"Yeah, so do I! I have spent ten years of wishing, praying, and searching to know that information," I explained. I have been very frustrated about it."

"I am beginning to understand your frustration," she said and called over another sister missionary to help.

The new assistant said something very profound. It was like lightning struck my brain in that moment. "Maybe we need to try looking at this in a different way. When was Sarah Tonge baptized a member of The Church of Jesus Christ of Latter-Day Saints?"

This question confused me. I hadn't really thought about it before. "I always thought she was baptized when she got married to James Sabey in her thirties. I think it was in the late 1890s, in Wallsburg, Utah."

"If we can trace Sarah's movements throughout her life, then we will be able to narrow down the time frame of when Maude was born and where Mr. Rose really was," the second sister missionary said.

This is why you ask questions of everyone you can. They might see a situation differently than you or know of a better way to go about researching a problem.

So, we started looking into the Tonge family's timeline, instead of Mr. Rose's timeline. The timelines had to have converged somewhere. The first sister missionary found the Tonges in Heber City, Wasatch County, Utah on the 1880 United States federal census.[10] The Tonges' surname is spelled Young instead of Tonge, but it was the same people who were on our original family group sheets—same given names, birth dates, and places. The misspelling could be because the person taking the census heard the name wrong and did not bother to ask for clarification. Censuses are riddled with errors; this is why other documents are needed to support or disprove them.

Transcript:

Name: Peter Young
Age: 36
Birth Date: Abt 1844
Birthplace: England
Home: in 1880, Heber, Wasatch, Utah, USA
Race: White
Gender: Male
Relation to Head of House: Self (Head)
Marital Status: Married

Spouse's Name: Elizabeth Young
Age: 34
Gender: Female
Father's Birthplace: England
Mother's Birthplace: England
Occupation: Farm laborer

Children:
Name: Sarah Young
Age: 15
Gender: Female

Name: Nancy Young
Age: 9
Gender: Female

Name: Margrete Young
Age: 5
Gender: Female

Name: Peter Young
Age: 2
Gender: Male

---

10 Ancestry, "United States Census 1880," database, *Ancestry*, (https://Ancestry.com: accessed 11 May 2019, entry for Peter Tonge (b. 1842), Heber City, Wasatch, Utah, USA, dist. 090, sudist. Blank: p. 1, fam. 10; "affiliated film number" 1339.

Unraveling the Family Secret

[7-296.]   A.
                                                                          313

Page No. 1
Supervisor's Dist. No. _____
Enumeration Dist. No. 90

Note A.—The Census Year begins June 1, 1879, and ends May 31, 1880.
Note B.—All persons will be included in the Enumeration who were living on the 1st day of June, 1880. No others will. Children BORN SINCE June 1, 1880, will be OMITTED. Members of Families who have DIED SINCE June 1, 1880, will be INCLUDED.
Note C.—Questions Nos. 13, 14, 22 and 23 are not to be asked in respect to persons under 10 years of age.

SCHEDULE 1.—Inhabitants in Heber City & Precinct, in the County of Wasatch, State of Utah enumerated by me on the 1st day of June, 1880.

Tho? H. Giles, Enumerator.

#	Family	Name	Race/Sex/Age	Relationship	Civil Cond.	Occupation	Health	Educ.	Birthplace	Father	Mother
1	1	Hatch Abram	W M 51		M	Farmer			Vermont	Vermont	Illinois
2		— Jane	W F 43	Wife	M	Keeping house			Pennsylvania	Iowa	New York
3		— Jane	W F 11	Daughter		at home		1	Utah	Vermont	Iowa
4		— Jaculine	W F 9	Daughter					Utah	Vermont	Iowa
5		Lott Amelia	W F 75	Mother in law					New York	New York	New York
6		Dodds Minnie A	W F 21	Daughter					Utah	Vermont	Iowa
7		Hatch Maria	W F 22	Daughter					Utah	England	Maine
8	2	Giles Thomas	W M 76		M	Farmer			England	England	England
9		— Veronica	W F 62	Wife	M	Keeping house			Scotland	Scotland	Scotland
10	3	Luke Harriett	W F 44			Keeping house		1	Maine	Maine	Maine
11		— Andrew	W M 20	Son		Farming			Utah	England	Maine
12		— Caroline	W F 18	Daughter		at home			Utah	England	Maine
13		— John H.	W M 15	Son		at home		1	Utah	England	Maine
14		— Mary Ann	W F 14	Daughter		at home			Utah	England	Maine
15		— Richard	W M 10	Son		at home			Utah	England	Maine
16	4	Howarth John	W M 51		M	Farmer			England	England	England
17		— Ann	W F 29	Wife	M	Keeping house			England	England	England
18		— John E.	W M 10	Son					Utah	England	England
19		— James A.	W M 3	Son					Utah	England	England
20		— Mary E.	W F 2	Daughter					Utah	England	England
21	5	Nordstrom John	W M 35		M	Shoe Maker			Sweden	Sweden	Sweden
22		— Charlotte	W F 29	Wife	M	Keeping house			Sweden	Sweden	Sweden
23		— Mary	W F 6	Daughter					Utah	Sweden	Sweden
24		— John C.	W M 5	Son					Utah	Sweden	Sweden
25		— Minnie	W F 3	Daughter					Utah	Sweden	Sweden
26		— Matilda	W F 1	Daughter					Utah	Sweden	Sweden
27	6	Hallbom Peter	W M 61		M	Tailor			Sweden	Sweden	Sweden
28		— Anne	W F 59	Wife	M	Keeping house			Sweden	Sweden	Sweden
29	7	Burgelin Victor	W M 21		M	Tailor			Sweden	Sweden	Sweden
30		— Mary	W F 26	Wife	M	Keeping house			Sweden	Sweden	Sweden
31	8	Meilam George B	W M 32		M	Farmer			Iowa	Iowa	Iowa
32		— Elenor B.	W F 29	Wife	M	Keeping house			England	England	England
33		— George W.	W M 8	Son					Utah	Iowa	England
34		— Francis J.	W M 6	Son					Utah	Iowa	England
35		— Oscar K.	W M 4	Son					Utah	Iowa	England
36		— Elenor	W F 2	Daughter					Utah	Iowa	England
37		— Sarah	W F 7/12	Daughter					Utah	Iowa	England
38	9	Street William	W M 30		M			1	England	England	England
39		— Ann	W F 22	Wife	M	Keeping house		1	England	England	England
40		— Mary H.	W F 5	Daughter					Wyoming	England	England
41		— Elizabeth	W F 4	Daughter					Wyoming	England	England
42		— William	W M 1	Son					Utah	England	England
43	→ 10	Young Peter	W M 36		M	Farm Laborer			England	England	England
44		— Elizabeth	W F 34	Wife	M	Keeping house		1 1	England	England	England
45		— Sarah	W F 16	Daughter				1	England	England	England
46		— Nancy	W F 9	Daughter				1	England	England	England
47		— Margret	W F 5	Daughter					Wyoming	England	England
48		— Peter	W M 2	Son					Wyoming	England	England
49		— Elizabeth	W F 4/12	Daughter					Utah	England	England
50		Sidago Elizabeth	W F 53	Boarding				1 1	England	England	England

Note D.—In making entries in columns 9, 10, 11, 12, 16 to 23, an affirmative mark only will be used—thus /, except in the case of divorced persons, column 11, when the letter "D" is to be used.
Note E.—Question No. 12 will only be asked in cases where an affirmative answer has been given either to question 10 or to question 11.
Note F.—Question No. 14 will only be asked in cases when a gainful occupation has been reported in column 13.
Note G.—In column 7 an abbreviation in the name of the month may be used, as Jan., Apr., Dec.

Name: *Elizabeth Young*
Age: *4½ Months*
Gender: *Female*

This was a revelation for me. My dad's side of the family had always insisted that the Tonges' first home after they arrived from England on the United States' Wyoming passenger ship in 1873, was American Fork, Utah County, Utah. (At this time, I still had no idea where the record of the ship was. FamilySearch has since found it for me.) The 1880 federal census proved that the Tonges lived in Heber City, Utah at one time.[11] Peter Tonge and his wife Elizabeth (Barnes) Tonge, the parents of Sarah Tonge, joined The Church of Jesus Christ of Latter-Day Saints while they were in England.

The sister missionaries suggested that I should look up the Tonges' church records for Heber City, Utah. There were two microfilm rolls to look at; that alone is a miracle.

Let me explain: There is only one place in the world where the Church of Jesus Christ of Latter-Day Saints' early church records are kept on microfilm. That is Salt Lake City, Utah, at the Family History Center. Living only an hour away from Salt Lake City was another miracle.

The new microfilm readers are so much smaller and easier to use. They are made to interface with a computer.[12] This makes it possible to print the images from the microfilm or save them as an image to a flash drive or to an email.

My whole journey—quest really—is one miracle after another. Searching through both films the first time turned up nothing.

A modern microfilm reader

While I took a lunch break downstairs in the break room, my mom took over for me. When I returned to my mom's side a half-hour later, she had not found anything either. We were not giving up hope, though. We knew we were supposed to be there that day to find something, anything, and I wasn't leaving until I had found it.

My mom went downstairs to eat, and I took over looking at the films again. I knew the Tonges' records were on those films. I just didn't understand why I wasn't finding them. After twenty more minutes, I was getting frustrated. I put my head down, took a few deep breaths, and said a silent prayer.

Dear Heavenly Father, I know I was sent here today to find stuff. I really do not care what I find. I just need to know if I am on the right track. You know I really try hard not to judge. I say these things in the name of Jesus Christ, Amen!

After gathering my thoughts, I started looking at the microfilm again. Not ten minutes later, I stopped on what looked like an index page in the middle of the microfilm. "Page 50, Tonge, Peter" was in the middle of the page. Excitement bubbled up in my chest. I couldn't believe my eyes. I nearly squealed in delight in the middle of the library. The records covered two pages.[13] On the last page, an absurd note was written next to their names: "In the 1890s whole family left in disgrace—incest."

---

11 Ancestry, "United States Census, 1880," database with images, *Ancestry,* (https://www.ancestry.com: accessed 22 May 2019) Year: 1880; Census Place: Heber, Wasatch, Utah; Roll: 1339; Page: 313A; Enumeration: 090.

12 "Picture of a Modern Microfilm Reader". Image Online, (https://www.bing.com/images/search?view=detailV2&ccid=CMHdzJdV&id=039B5B-330810C6C373F464304FAB2F4E7381533E&thid=OIP.CMHdzJdVzjNB7EzupdgGvgHaFY&mediaurl=https://www.stimaging.com/wp-content/uploads/microfilm-scanner-viewscan-4-smal1l.png&q=microfilm%20reader&ck=AA9B202E0A931B5A63FB346412F3CD13&idpp=rc&id-pview=singleimage&form=rc2idp : Accessed 2 August 2024.)

13 FamilySearch Family History Library of the Church of Jesus Christ of Latter-Day Saints, "The Church of Jesus Christ of Latter-Day Saints Membership records, U.S.A. and Canada; Heber East Ward Records of Members Early 1902" images, *Family History Library,* (FHL, Salt Lake City, Utah: Accessed 11 May 2019), Church records of the Tonges, Libr. No. 13271, Microfilm Number 0026026, About Page 51.

No.	NAME	PARENTS' NAMES		BIRTH			BLESSING		FIRST BAPTISM		FIRST CONFIRMATION	
		FATHER'S Name	MOTHER'S Maiden Name	Day Month Year	Town	County	State or Nation	Day Month Year	By Whom	Day Month Year	By Whom	Day Month Year
	Phipps Ellis R. Olea		Ellis R.		Salt Lake City	Salt Lake	Utah					
	Tonge Peter	Robert Tonge	Sarah Greening	7 Sep 1832	Bolton	Lancashire	England			1869 J. Sowers		1869 J.
	Tonge Elizabeth	Thomas Barnes	Nancy Boardman	1 Jan 1842						1852 G. Lyons		1852
	Tonge Sarah	Peter Tonge	Elizabeth Barnes	17 Sep 1868					1868 A. Forter	1872 S. Peter		1872 S. Peter
	Tonge Nancy	"	"	2 Mar 1869	Farnworth				1869 J. Sowers			
	Tonge Nancy Ellen	"	"	8 Jan 1871					1871 S. Legge	28 Aug 1881 Joseph Moulton	28 Aug 1881 Jo. Todd	
	Tonge Margaret Alice	"	"	18 July 1874	Evanstown	Uintah	Wyoming		Aug 1874 Morris			
	Tonge Peter Jr.	"	"	2 June 1876					March 1877 Burton			
	Tonge Mary Elizabeth	"	"	2 Feb 1879	Park City	Summit	Utah		Feb 1881 J. Horricks			
	Tonge Thomas Edward	"	"	15 Nov 1881	Heber	Wasatch	"		2 " 1881 Jos. Hatken			
	Thomas Charles	Charles Thomas	Elizabeth Carter	14 Sep 1859			England					
	Thomas Emeline	Richard Sessions	Lucretia W.	1 May 1860			Illinois					
	Thomas Charles Richard	Charles Thomas	Emeline Sessions	4 Jan 1881	Heber	Wasatch	Utah	21 Jan 1881 John M. Murdock			

SAINTS, OF THE East Heber WARD Wasatch STAKE OF ZION.

ORDINATION				RE-BAPTISM			RE-CONFIRMATION			RECEIVED		REMOVED		DIED		REMARKS
Day	Month	Year	By Whom	To What Office	Day Month Year	By Whom	Day Month Year	By Whom	Day Month Year	Where From	Day Month Year	Where To	Day Month Year			
										Oct 1871 Salt Lake City	May 1873 Salt Lake City			Known as Teacher in School
										April 1873						
1871 H. Priest		Elder	11 Mar 1873 Wm Clegg	11 Mar 1873 R.S. Welch				About 1880 whole family	recovered under disgrace issued			
				11 Mar 1873 Wm Clegg	11 Mar 1873 Rob Broadhead				1880 Oak Haven			
									1878			

Jubilee Haddessa

Transcript:

RECORD OF THE MEMBERS OF THE CHURCH OF JESUS CHRIST OF LATTER-DAY SAINTS, OF THE EAST HEBER WARD WASATCH STAKE OF ZION

Name: Tonge, Peter
Parents' names: Father: Tonge, Robert; Mother: Deerding, Sarah
Birthdate and place: 7 September 1843; Bolton, Lancashire, England
First baptism: 1869, J. Fowell
First confirmation: 1869, J. Fowell
Ordination: 1870, H. Bidell, elder
Re-Baptism: 22 March 1883, William Clegg
Re-Confirmation: 11 March 1883, Ronald Broadhead
Removed: About 1890, whole family
Remarks: Removed under disgrace—incest

Name: Tonge, Elizabeth
Parents' names: Father: Barnes, Thomas; Mother: Bordman, Nancy
Birthdate and place: 2 November 1845; Bolton, Lancashire, England
First baptism: 1855, G. Lyons
First confirmation: 1855
Re-Baptism: 22 March 1883, William Clegg
Re-Confirmation: 11 March 1883, Ronald Broadhead
Removed:
Died: 1898
Remarks: Died, Heber

Name: Tonge, Sarah
Parents' names: Father: Tonge, Peter; Mother: Barnes, Elizabeth
Birthdate and place: 17 September 1864; Bolton, Lancashire, England
Blessing date: 1864, A. Fortie
First baptism: 1875, S. Tike
First confirmation: 1875, S. Tike

Name: Tonge, Nancy
Parents' names: Father: Tonge, Peter; Mother: Barnes, Elizabeth
Birthdate and place: 2 March 1869; Fernworth, Lancashire, England
Blessing date: 1869, J. Fowell

Name: Tonge, Nancy Ellen
Parents' names: Father: Tonge, Peter; Mother: Barnes, Elizabeth
Birthdate and place: 8 January 1872; Fernworth, Lancashire, England
Blessing date: 1872, T. Legga
First baptism: 28 August 1881, Joseph Moulten
First confirmation: 28 August 1881, Tho. Toss

Name: Tonge, Margaret Alice
Parents' names: Father: Tonge, Peter; Mother: Barnes, Elizabeth
Birthdate and place: 18 July 1876; Evanston, Uintah, Wyoming
Blessing date: August 1876, Morris

Name: Tonge, Peter Jr.
Parents' names: Father: Tonge, Peter; Mother: Barnes, Elizabeth
Birthdate and place: 8 January 1878; Evanston, Uintah, Wyoming
Blessing date: March 1878, Burton

Name: Tonge, Mary Elizabeth
Parents' names: Father: Tonge, Peter; Mother: Barnes, Elizabeth
Birthdate and place: 2 February 1880; Park City, Summit, Utah
Blessing date: February 1881, J. Horricks

Name: Tonge, Thomas Edward
Parents' names: Father: Tonge, Peter; Mother: Barnes, Elizabeth
Birthdate and place: 15 November 1881; Heber, Wasatch, Utah
Blessing date: 2 February 1882, Tho. Hicken

I stared at that glaring note for over five minutes, trying to comprehend it. There were so many emotions raging in my chest. I remembered my father mentioning something years ago along the lines of Peter Tonge may have fathered a child with his daughter Sarah. It was just some family rumor, and I dismissed it at the time. Apparently, I had filed this knowledge away in the back of my mind.

Another sister missionary came up to me and asked me if I had found anything. I showed her what I had found. Three sister missionaries, in all, helped me that day. I do not remember any of their names, I will be forever grateful for their help that day.

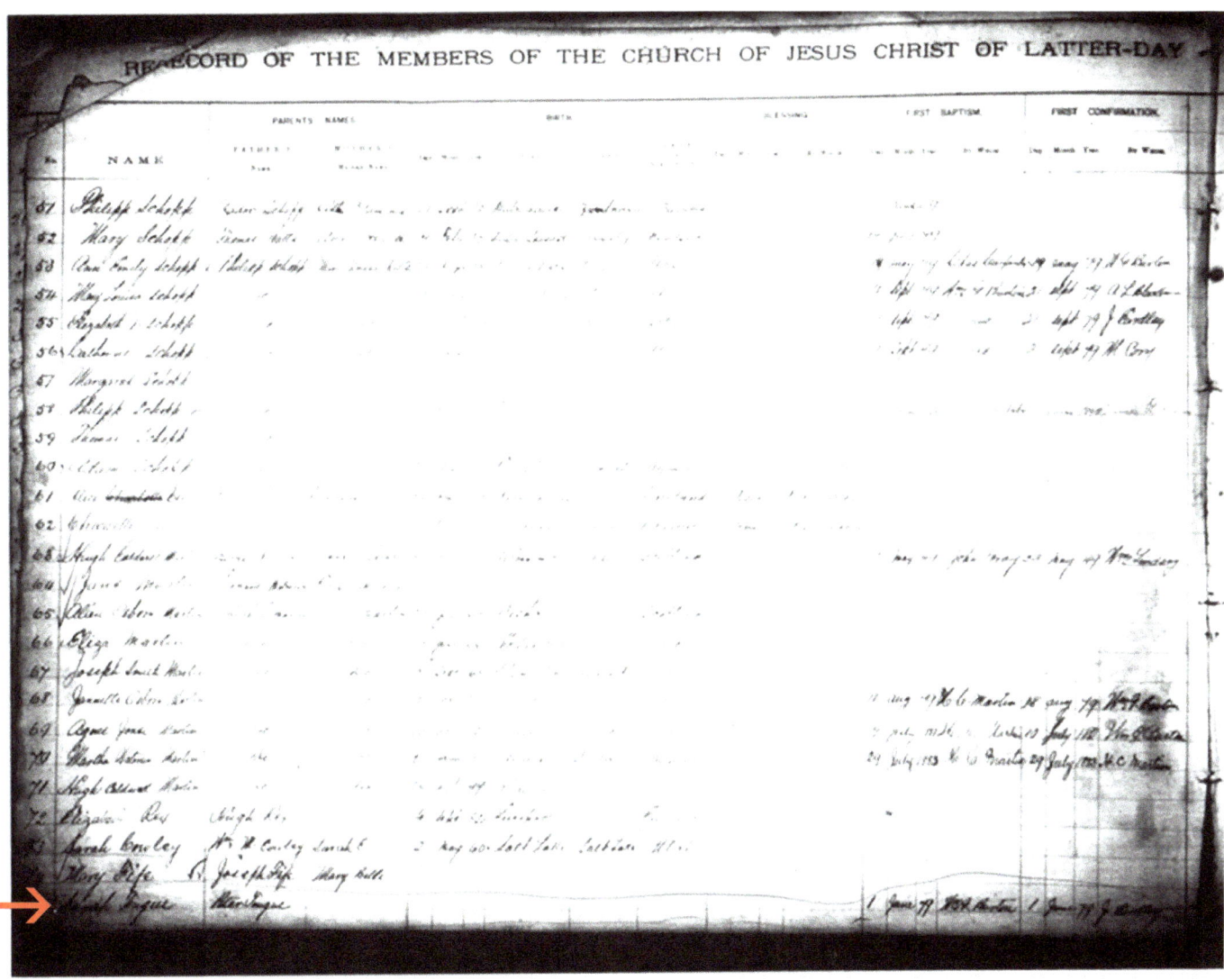

"I am a little conflicted by this . . . there is a family rumor about this. It's sad that my dad's side of the family saw this and decided not to look further into it. What if it's wrong? What if someone started rumors about the Tonges and ruined their lives?"

"This has just made you want to investigate this deeper, hasn't it? This would also explain why no one wanted to talk about it," the sister missionary said.

"Yeah, look. Some of the Tonge children were born in Evanston, Wyoming. Do you have church records for Evanston?"

We went and found the microfilm of the early church records for Evanston. I started looking for the Tonges' church records, and discovered the baptismal record of Sarah Tonge as a member of the Church of Jesus Christ of Latter-Day Saints.[14]

Transcript:
Name: *Sarah Tonge*
Father: *Peter Tonge*
Baptized: *1 June 1879*
By: *Wm J Burton*
Confirmation: *1 June 1879*
By: *J. Bradley*

---

14 FamilySearch Family History Library of the Church of Jesus Christ of Latter-Day Saints, "The Church of Jesus Christ of Latter-Day Saints Membership records, U.S.A. and Canada, Evanston, WY Ward Records of Members," images, Family History Library, (FHL, Salt Lake City: Accessed 11 May 2119), Sarah Tonge's Baptismal Record, (1 June 1879) -1877 Evanston, WY Microfilm Number: 034547 About Page 10 bottom of the page.

She was fifteen years old when she was baptized a member of The Church of Jesus Christ of Latter-Day Saints.

There was also a note on that record: "Record removed to Park City, 1880."

This proves that the Tonges moved to Utah in 1880. This also proves that the Tonges' first home after joining the Church of Jesus Christ of Latter-Day Saints in England and coming over the Atlantic Ocean was Evanston, Wyoming—not American Fork, Utah.

Court Cases of Peter and Sarah Tonge

There was a lot of information to process after the discoveries that day at the library. I had to go home and try to make sense of everything that I had learned. My mom was impressed at what I had found. She, too, was mulling things over. The drive home was quiet.

My friend, Nicole and I attended church the next day, and I told her about what I had found out the day before. My friend had an epiphany about the incest investigation. "I wonder if there are court cases for this."

Brilliant! A few minutes later, we had found the court cases of Peter Tonge and Sarah Tonge on FamilySearch.[15]

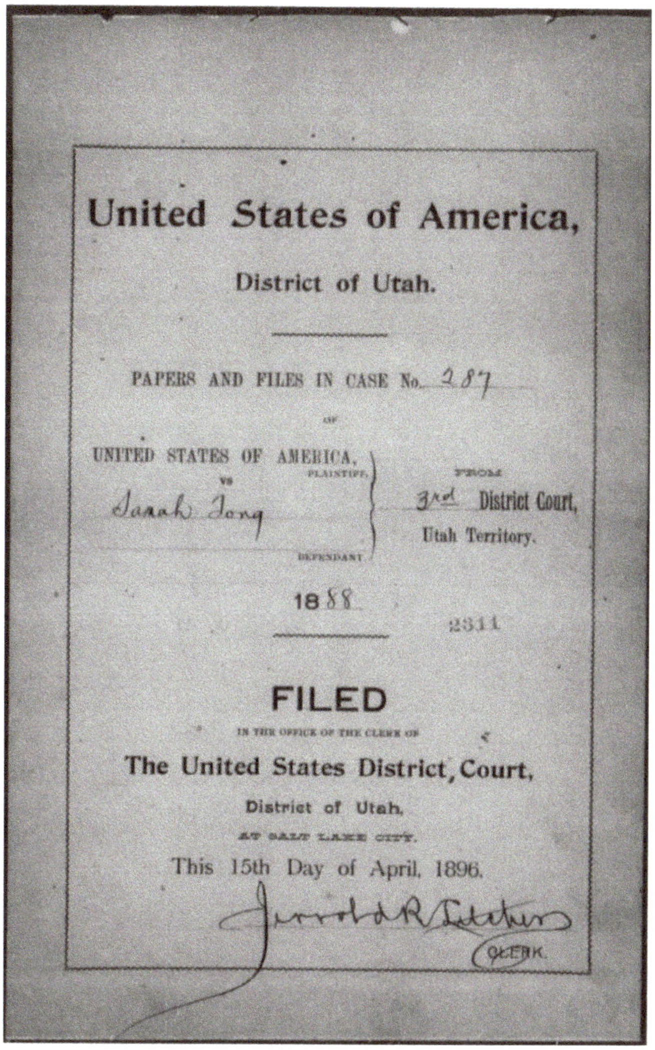

Transcript:

United States of America.
District of Utah.
Papers and Files in Case No. 287 Of United States of America, plaintiff, Vs. Sarah Tong, defendant
From 3rd District Court, Utah Territory, 1888
2311
FILED
In the office of the clerk of The United States District, Court, District of Utah At Salt Lake City.
This is 15th Day of April, 1896.
Jarrol R. Liteher (Spelling unclear), Clerk

---

15 Fold3, "Utah, Territorial Case Files of the U.S. District Courts, 1870-1896," images, Fold3 database, (https://www.familysearch.org: accessed 12 May 2019), Court Case of Peter Tonge (24 Feb 1888), Court Case Number 2310, Microfilm#: M1401, National Archives and Records Administration, 1987, Roll 32. "Utah, Territorial Case Files of the U.S. District Courts, 1870-1896," images, *Fold3 database*, (https://www.familysearch.org: accessed 12 May 2019), Court Case of Sarah Tonge (24 Feb 1888), Court Case Number 2311, Microfilm# M1401 National Archives and Records Administration, 1987, Roll 32.

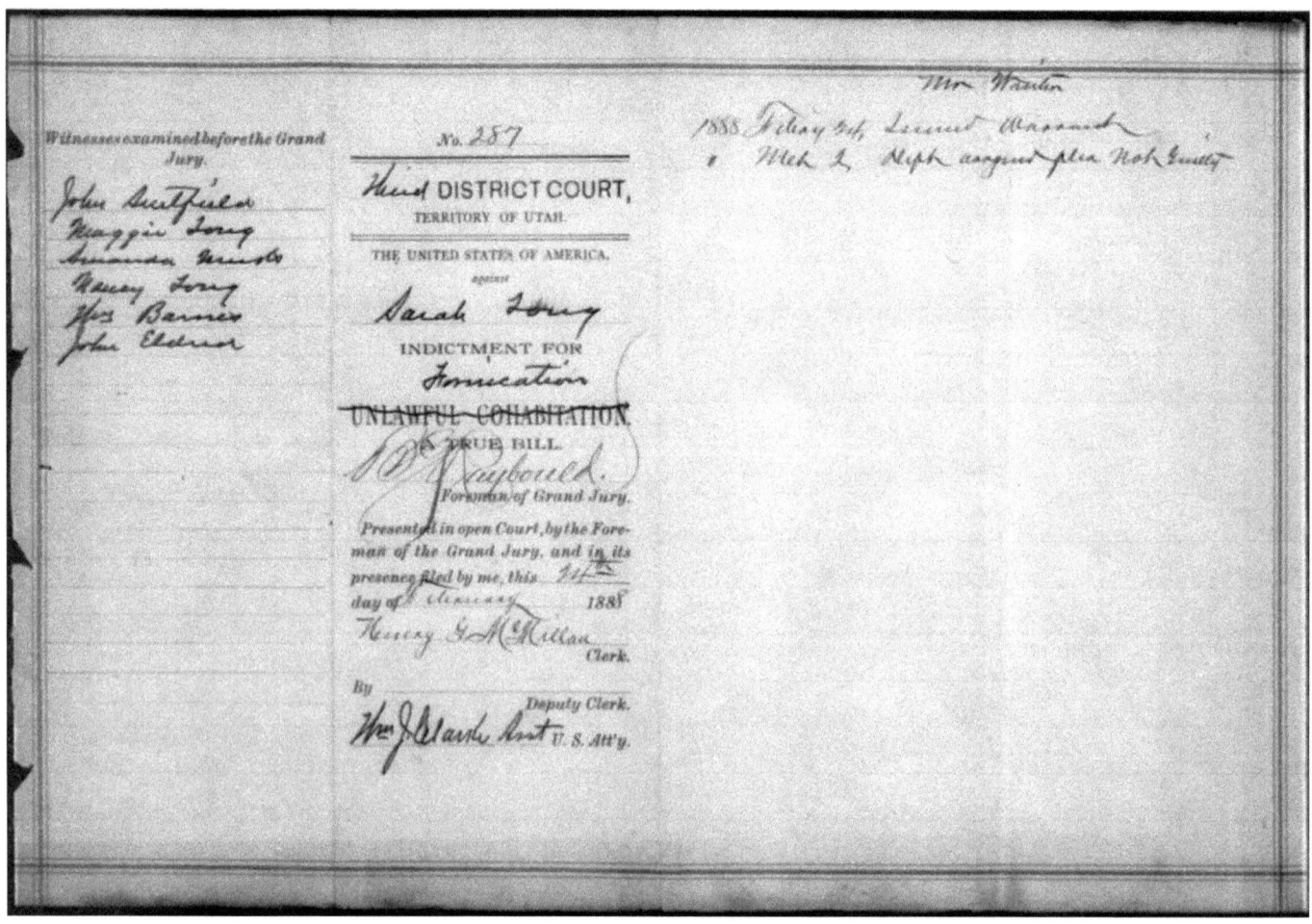

Witnesses examined before the Grand Jury.
John Swetfield
Maggie Tong
Amanda Musto?
Nancy Tong
Wm Barnes
John Elder?

No. 287
Third DISTRICT COURT
Territory of Utah
The United States of America Against Sarah Tong
INDICTMENT FOR Fornication
UNLAWFUL COHOBITATION
A True Bill.
P. K.? Raybould, Foreman of Grand Jury
  Presented in open court, by foreman of the Grand Jury, and in its presence pled by me, this 24th day of February 1888
Henrey G McMillan, Clerk
Wm J. Wanter, Ast. U.S. Att'y

Mr. Wanter
1888, February 24, Incest Warrant
1888, March 2, heph?
Arrgrand? plea Not Guilty (Unsure of wording)

United States of America,
TERRITORY OF UTAH, } ss. No. _____
Third JUDICIAL DISTRICT.

In the *third* Judicial District, in and for the Territory of Utah, within the United States of America, of the term of *February* in the year of our Lord, one thousand eight hundred and eighty-*Eight*.

THE UNITED STATES OF AMERICA,

Against

Sarah Long

The Grand Jurors of the United States of America, within and for the district aforesaid, at the term and in the Territory aforesaid, being duly empanelled, sworn and charged, on their oaths do find and present that *Sarah Long* late of said district, heretofore, to-wit: on the *first* day of *June* in the year of our Lord one thousand eight hundred and eighty-*seven*, in the said district, Territory aforesaid, and within the jurisdiction of this court, ~~and on divers days thereafter~~ ~~...~~ ~~...~~ she the said Sarah Long being then and there an unmarried woman did unlawfully commit fornication with one Peter Long, by then and there having carnal knowledge of the body of him the said Peter Long —

against the form of the statute of the said United States, in such case made and provided, and against the peace and dignity of the same.

S. W. Raybould
Foreman of Grand Jury.

William J. Lelansh
Assistant U. S. District Attorney.

Jubilee Haddessa

United States of America,
TERRITORY OF UTAH
Third JUDICIAL DISTRICT

In the Third Judicial District, in and for the Territory of Utah, within the United States of America, of the term of February in the year of our Lord, one thousand eight hundred and eighty-eight.
THE UNITED STATES OF AMERICA Against Sarah Tong

The Grand Jurors of United States of America, within and for the district aforesaid, at the term and in the Territory aforesaid, being duly empaneled, sworn and charged on their oaths do find and present that Sarah Tong late of said District, heretofore, to-wit: on the First day of June in the year of our Lord one thousand eight hundred and eighty-seven, in the said District. Territory aforesaid, and within the jurisdiction of the court.

She, the said Sarah Tong, being there and then an unmarried woman did unlawfully commit fortification with one Peter Tong by him and then having carnal knowledge of the body of him, the said Peter Tong.

Against the form of the statute of the United States, in such case made and provided, and against the peace and dignity of the same.
P.J.? Raybould, Foreman of the Jury
William J. Wanter, Assistant U.S. Attorney

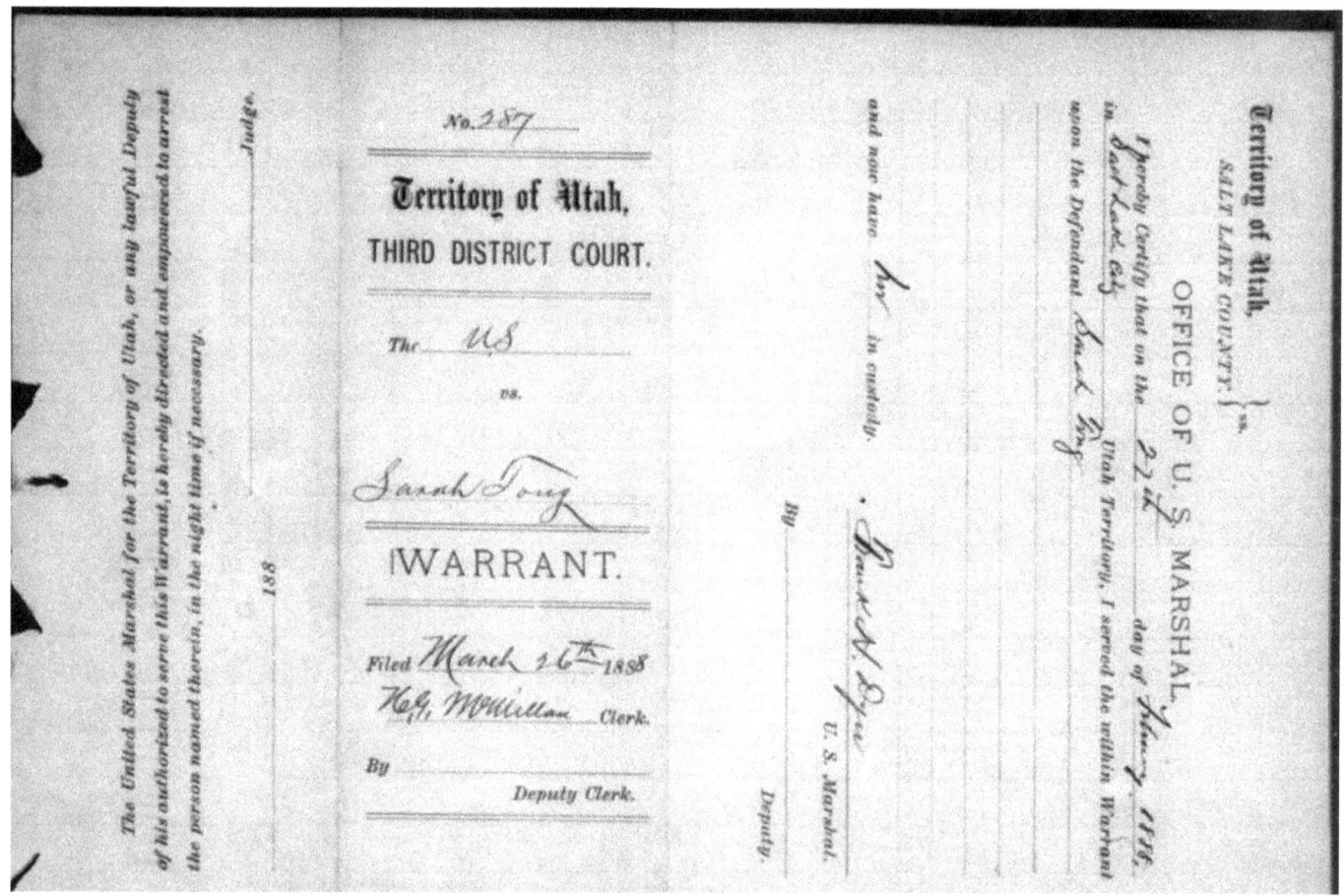

The United States Marshal for the Territory of Utah, or any lawful Deputy of his authorized to serve the Warrant, is hereby directed and empowered to arrest the person named therein, in the night time if necessary.

No. 287
Territory of Utah
THIRD DISTRICT COURT
The U.S. Vs. Sarah Tong
WARRANT

Filed March 26th 1888
H.G. McMillan, Clerk
Territory of Utah
SALT LAKE COUNTY
OFFICE OF U.S. MARSHAL

I hereby Certify that on the 22th day of February 1888, in Salt Lake City, Utah Territory, I served the within Warrant upon the Defendant Sarah Tong and now have her in custody.

Frank H. Dyer, U. S. Marshal

IN THE DISTRICT COURT OF THE THIRD JUDICIAL DISTRICT

OF THE

TERRITORY OF UTAH.

The People of the United States of America, in the Territory of Utah,

To the U. S. Marshal for said Territory, Greeting:

An Indictment having been found on the 24th day of February A. D. eighteen hundred and eighty-eight in the District Court for the Third Judicial District in and for the Territory of Utah, charging Sarah Tong with the crime of Fornication

You are therefore commanded to forthwith arrest the above named Sarah Tong and bring her before that Court, to answer said indictment, or if the Court has adjourned for the term, that you keep, or cause her to be safely kept in custody until the further order of this Court; or if she require it, that you take her before A. G. Norrell U. S. Commissioner, to be admitted to bail in the sum of $500.00

C. S. Zane, Judge.

WITNESS my hand and the seal of said Court, affixed at Salt Lake City, this 24th day of February A. D. 1888

Henry G. McMillan
Clerk.

By _____ Deputy Clerk.

IN THE DISTRICT COURT OF THE THIRD JUDICIAL DISTRICT OF THE TERRITORY OF UTAH.
The People of the United States of America in the Territory of Utah
To the U. S. Marshal for said Territory, Greeting:

An Indictment having been found on the 24th day of February A. D. eighteen hundred and eighty-eight in the District Court for the Third Judicial District in and for the Territory of Utah, charging Sarah Tong with the crime of Fornication.

You are therefore commanded to forthwith arrest the above named Sarah Tong and bring her before that Court, to answer said indictment, or if the Court has adjourned for the term, that you keep, or cause her to be safely kept in custody until the further order of this Court; or if She require it, that you take her before A. G. Nornell U.S. Commissioner, to be admitted to bail in the sum of $500.00.
C. S. Zane
WITNESS my hand and the seal of said court, affixed
At Salt Lake City,
this 24th day of February A. D. 1888
Henrey G. McMillan, Clerk

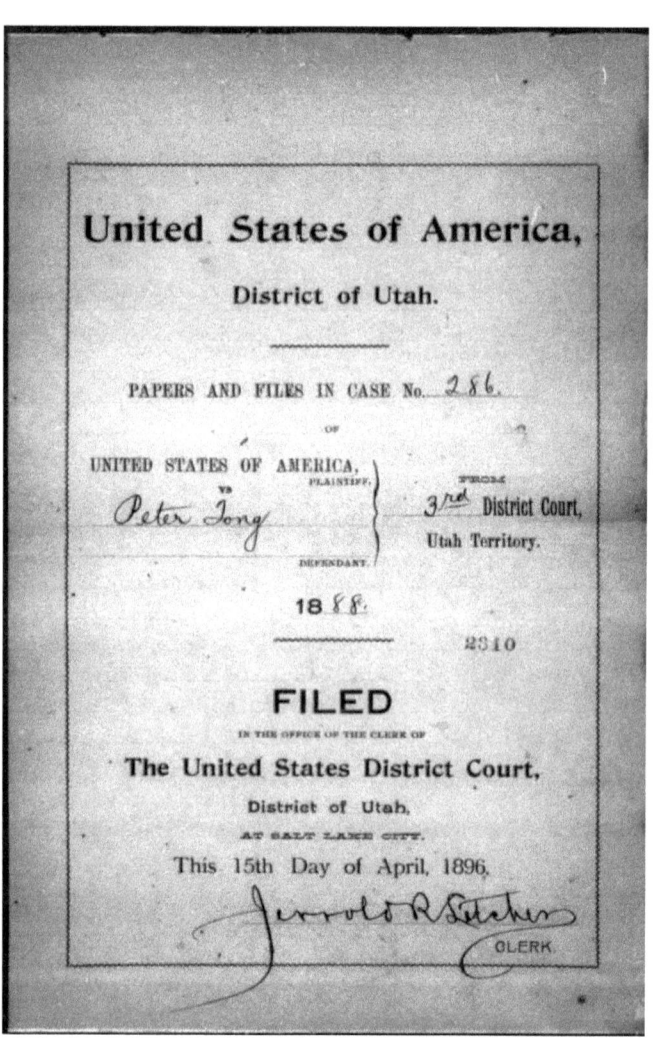

Peter Tonge's Court Case

Transcript:

United States of America, District of Utah
PAPERS AND FILES IN CASE NO. 286 Of
UNITED STATES OF AMERICA, Plaintiff Vs. Peter Tong, Defendant
From 3rd District Court, Utah Territory.
1888
2310
FILED
IN THE OFFICE OF THE CLERK OF The United States District Court District of Utah AT SALT LAKE CITY,
This 15th Day of April, 1896.
Gerrold R. Litcher, Clerk

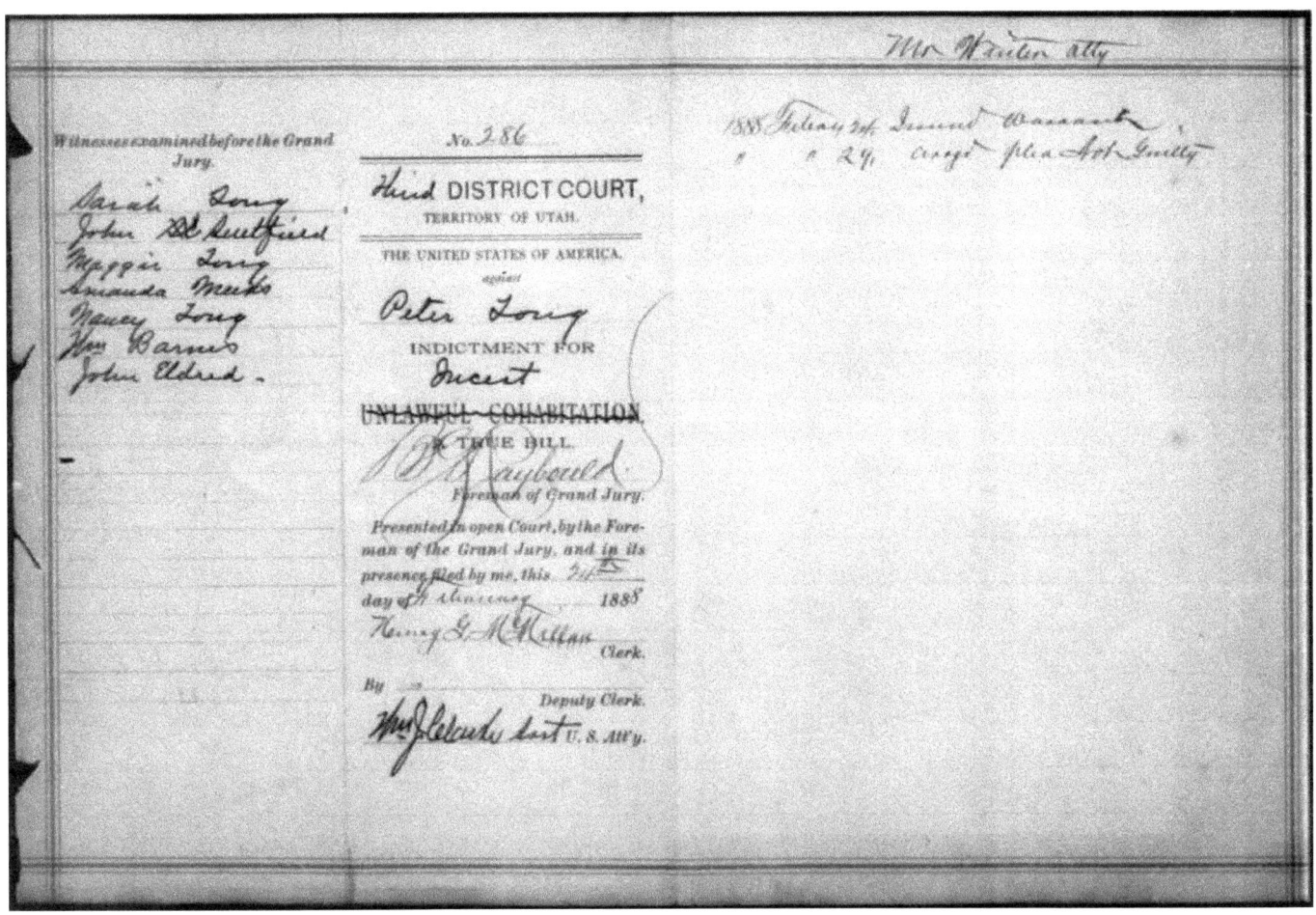

Witnesses examined before the Grand Jury:
Sarah Tong
John Suitfield
Maggie Tong
Amanda Murbo?
Nancy Tong
Wm Barnes
John Elder

No. 286
Third District Court, TERRITORY OF UTAH
The United States Against Peter Tong
INDICTMENT FOR INCEST

~~UNLAWFUL COHABITATION~~
A TRUE BILL
P. J.? Raybould, Foreman of Grand Jury
Presented in open court, by the Foreman of the Grand Jury, and in its presence filed by me, this 24th day of February 1888.
Henrey G. McMillan, Clerk
Wm J. Wanter, Asst. U.S. Att'y.

Mr. Wanter, Atty
1888 February 24, Incest Warrant
1888 February 24, arrgt. Plea Not Guilty (unsure of wording)

United States of America,
TERRITORY OF UTAH, ss. No. _____
Third JUDICIAL DISTRICT.

In the third Judicial District, in and for the Territory of Utah, within the United States of America, of the term of February in the year of our Lord, one thousand eight hundred and eighty-eight.

THE UNITED STATES OF AMERICA,

Against

Peter Long

The Grand Jurors of the United States of America, within and for the district aforesaid, at the term and in the Territory aforesaid, being duly empanelled, sworn and charged, on their oaths do find and present that Peter Long late of said district, heretofore, to-wit: on the first day of June in the year of our Lord one thousand eight hundred and eighty seven, in the said district, Territory aforesaid, and within the jurisdiction of this court, ~~[struck through]~~

did unlawfully have sexual intercourse with one Sarah Long, she the said Sarah Long being then and there the daughter of him the said Peter Long, and he the said Peter Long then and there well knew.

against the form of the statute of the said United States, in such case made and provided, and against the peace and dignity of the same.

F. J. Raybould
Foreman of Grand Jury.

William J. Leverich
Assistant U. S. District Attorney.

United States of America,
TERRITORY OF UTAH.
Third JUDICIAL COURT.

In the Third Judicial Court, in and for the Territory of Utah, within the United States of America, of the term of February in the year of our Lord, one thousand eight hundred and eighty-eight.

THE UNITED STATES OF AMERICA Against Peter Tong

The Grand Jurors of the United States of America, within and for the district aforesaid, at the term and in the Territory aforesaid, being duly empaneled, sworn, and charged, on their oaths do find and present that Peter Tong late of said district, heretofore, to-wit: on the First day of June in the year of our Lord one thousand and eighty-seven, in the said district, Territory aforesaid, and within the jurisdiction of this court, Did unlawfully have sexual intercourse with one Sarah Tong. She, the said Sarah Tong, being then and there the daughter of him, the said Peter Tong, and he, the said Peter Tong, then and there ..... know.

Against the form of the statute of the United States, in such case made and provided, and against the peace and dignity of the same.

P.J.? Raybould, Foreman of the Jury
William J. Wanter, Assistant U.S. Attorney

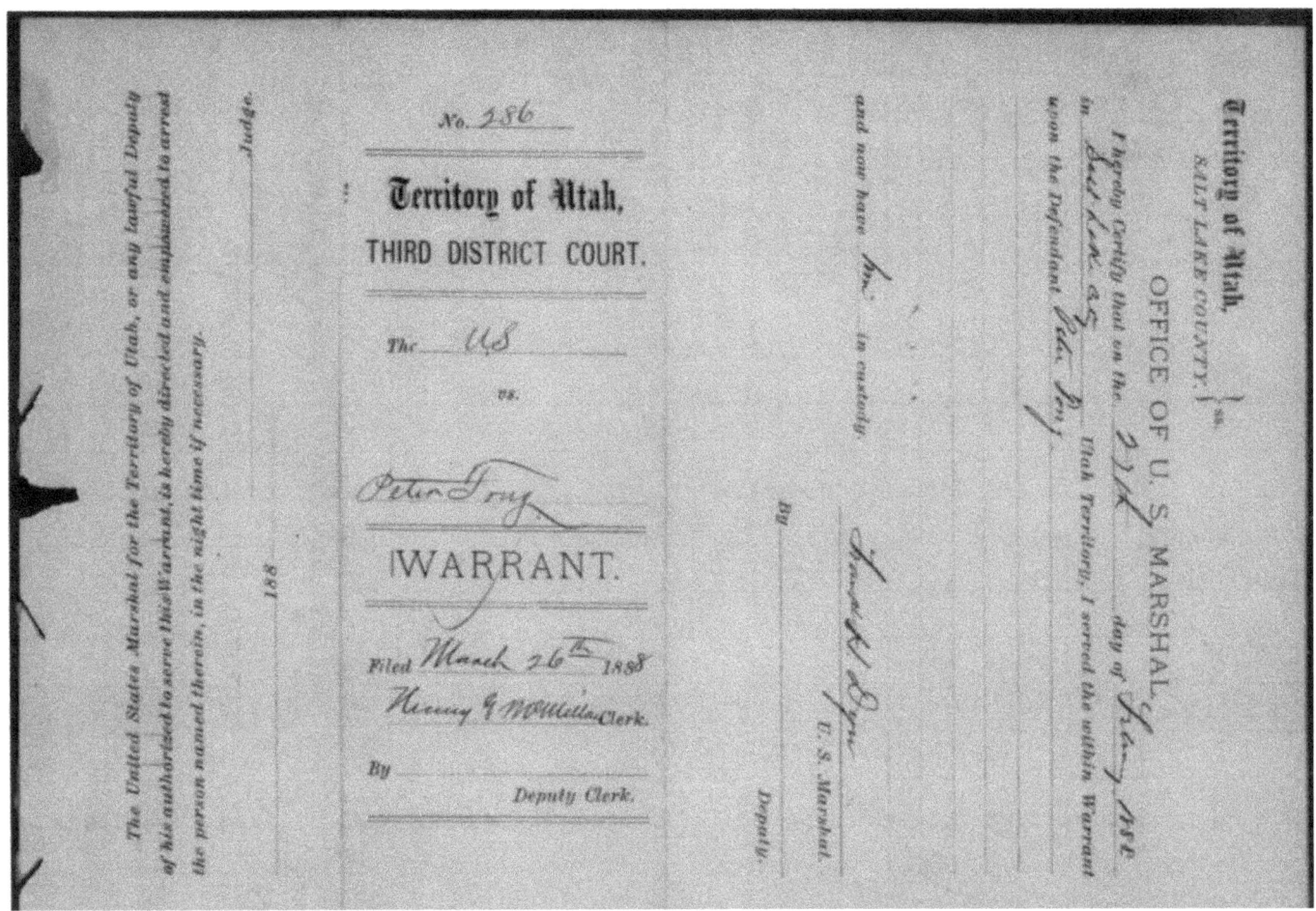

The United States Marshal for the Territory of Utah, or any lawful Deputy of his authorized to serve the Warrant, is hereby directed and empowered to arrest the person named therein, in the night time if necessary.

No. 286
Territory of Utah
THIRD DISTRICT COURT
The U.S. Vs. Peter Tong
WARRANT

Filed March 26th 1888
H.G. McMillan, Clerk
Territory of Utah
SALT LAKE COUNTY
OFFICE OF U.S. MARSHAL

I hereby Certify that on the 22th day of February 1888, in Salt Lake City, Utah Territory, I served the within Warrant upon the Defendant Sarah Tong and now have her in custody.

Frank H. Dyer, U. S. Marshal

IN THE DISTRICT COURT OF THE THIRD JUDICIAL DISTRICT
OF THE
TERRITORY OF UTAH.

The People of the United States ~~in the Territory of Utah~~ of America,

To the U. S. Marshal for said Territory, Greeting:

An Indictment having been found on the 24th day of February A. D. eighteen hundred and eighty-eight in the District Court for the Third Judicial District in and for the Territory of Utah, charging

Peter Tong

with the crime of Incest

You are therefore commanded to forthwith arrest the above named Peter Tong and bring him before that Court, to answer said indictment, or if the Court has adjourned for the term, that you keep, or cause him to be safely kept in custody until the further order of this Court; or if he require it, that you take him before A. G. Norrell U. S. Commissioner, to be admitted to bail in the sum of $1000.00

C. S. Zane, Judge.

WITNESS my hand and the seal of said Court, affixed at Salt Lake City, this 24th day of February A. D. 1888

Henry G. McMillan, Clerk.

By _____ Deputy Clerk.

IN THE DISTRICT COURT OF THE THIRD JUDICIAL DISTRICT OF THE TERRITORY OF UTAH.

The People of the United States of America in the Territory of Utah,

To the U. S. Marshal for said Territory, Greeting:

An Indictment having been found on the 24th day of February A. D. eighteen hundred and eighty-eight in the District Court for the Third Judicial District in and for the Territory of Utah, charging Peter Tong With the crime of Incest

You are therefore commanded to forthwith arrest the above named Peter Tong and bring him before that Court, to answer said indictment, or if the Court has adjourned for the term, that you keep, or cause he to be safely kept in custody until the further order of this Court; or if he require it, that you take him before A. G. Nornell U.S. Commissioner, to be admitted to bail in the sum of $1000.00.

C. S. Zane

WITNESS my hand and the seal of said court, affixed At Salt Lake City, this 24th day of February A. D. 1888

Henrey G. McMillan, Clerk

Their surname was spelled Tong instead of Tonge. These documents showed that Sarah's two sisters, Maggie Tong and Nancy Tong, were witnesses. The court cases also prove that Peter and Sarah were innocent. They were both exonerated.

Sarah's bail was set at $500. In 2024 money, this is $16,502.53. Peter's bail was $1,000. In 2024 money, that is $33,005.06. These sums are a lot of money, then and now. Law enforcement really didn't want Sarah or Peter to get out of jail.

These court documents led to so many more leads and ideas to follow and explore: Newspaper articles and a return to the Family History Center. There, I would investigate more on Peter and Sarah's court cases and the idea that Mr. Rose had to be in the Utah Territorial Penitentiary at the same time as Sarah in order for them to conceive Maude. All the leads I had to run down were exhilarating! This was more leads than I had ever collected. I felt like I was very close to finding out who Mr. Rose and Mr. Spratley were after a decade of searching.

The Monday after my friend and I found the court cases, I went to lunch with one of my co-workers. (She is a good friend of mine now). She asked me what I had done over the weekend.

I told her about my adventure to the Family History Center in Salt Lake City, the incest note, and the court cases I had found. We discussed how rumors can destroy lives.

"This sounds like a Hollywood movie," she said.

"Well, it may have to be a book first," I replied.

At the time, I thought we were only joking around. However, that was becoming more of a reality every day.

Newspaper Articles

Several newspaper articles reference Sarah and Peter Tonge. They are about their arrests and some of their experiences in the Utah Territorial Penitentiary. These two were in every major newspaper of the time. They were celebrities, but not in a good way. It would be like being on every major news outlet today for a scandal.

The article that was invaluable to me was titled "The Incest Cases."[16]

The Incest Cases.

The trial of Peter Tong, of Summit County, on the charge of incest with his daughter Sarah, took place in the Third District Court yesterday afternoon, and resulted in the acquittal of the defendant, the jury being out about four hours. His daughter testified that a young man named Gerrold, with whom she had been keeping company, was the father of the child. This morning the case against Sarah Tong, for incest, was dismissed, on motion of the district attorney, and the defendant has been set at liberty.

This May 2, 1888, article told me that the Tonges—though Tonge is spelled Tong in this article—were living in Summit County, Utah at the time.

There was indeed a baby involved, and the people of Summit County thought the baby's father was Peter, Sarah's father. Sarah testified that the baby's father was a young man by the name of Gerrold.

Both Sarah and Peter were acquitted of the crime of incest and set free. I have not found any information on this Gerrold. I believe that Sarah just threw out a random name to protect her father and the man she was truly seeing, her secret lover.

Another article—"For Incest," February 8, 1888—told me a little bit more about the baby.[17]

For Incest.

Miss Tonge, who is under arrest on the charge of incest, was brought down from Park City today by Deputy Marshal Vandercook, and will be placed in the penitentiary, where Peter Tonge, her father, and the reputed father of her child, is now being held for trial. The infant, which is about two weeks old, is terribly deformed, and presents a sickening sight.

The child was about two weeks old and deformed. The year was 1888; people did not understand that babies could be born deformed for many reasons. Birth defects happen all the time, even now in the 2020s. Back then in 1888, birth defects were explained away as the mother must have been a bad person. Or in Sarah Tonge's case, her disabled baby was so-called proof of her engaging in an incestuous relationship with her father.

In reality, it could have been any number of factors during the time period: "Medications" that were really poisonous, living near and around the silver mines, malnutrition of the mother, etc.

---

16 Newspapers, "The Incest Case," images, *Newspaper database*, (http://www.newspaper.com: accessed 27 May 2019) Peter Tonge and Sarah Tonge (2 May 1888), Deseret News (Salt Lake City, Utah), 2 May 1888, Wed. - Page 4

17 Newspapers, "For Incest," images, *Newspaper database*, (http://www.newspapers.com: accessed 27 May 2019), Peter and Sarah Tonge, The Salt Lake Herald (Salt Lake City, Utah), 8 Feb. 1888, Tue. - Page 3.

I have recently read a book by Gary Kimball that discussed a Chinatown neighborhood in old town Park City, Summit County, Utah, in the 1800s.[18] Gary talked about how the people of Park City, both residents and the miners, treated the Chinese men so badly. Racism at its ugly core is fear, determining that anyone and anything that is different from your culture is inferior. Our differences make us stronger; the same is true about learning from one another. Kimball wrote that they would experiment on these Chinese men because they were different, so what would stop people from experimenting on a lady who wasn't in her right mind and who just happened to be pregnant at the time? My point is that these prejudices, rumors, and hatred only saw a poor sickly child as a product of incest because, by gosh, there couldn't be any other explanation. Rumors can destroy people's lives today, and they could do the same thing more than a hundred years ago.

The more I learn about Sarah Tonge, the more I believe she had bipolar disorder.[19] My father was diagnosed with bipolar disorder about fifteen years ago. Bipolar disorder can be hereditary, and we had no idea where it had come from in the family—until now. One of the symptoms of bipolar disorder is hypersexism, also called having a very high libido. A person would want sex all the time. Something happened to Sarah around the time she and her family were living in Utah to trigger her bipolar disorder. She started sleeping around, it appears, and the papers even painted her as "crazy lady" or an "interesting lady."

She might have become a prostitute in Park City to satisfy her sexual urges from her mental illness. Plus, prostitution was one of the only ways women could make money for thousands of years. It is all just so sad.

Bipolar disorder can be triggered by trauma or grief. Sarah Tonge's bipolar disorder might have been triggered by her mother, Elizabeth Barnes Tonge, passing away five years before she and her father ended up in prison for incest in 1888.[20]

The more I learn about Peter Tonge, the more I think he was accused of something he never did. People, as always, hated what was different or couldn't be explained. Or, perhaps someone wanted the land the Tonges owned. Looking through all the evidence, he seemed to be the only one to stand up for Sarah. He was the only person who never left her side, the only one who always had Sarah's back throughout her life. He was doing what he thought was right—protecting his disturbed daughter. What is right and what is the law are not always the same thing.

Another article, "Committed to Jail," states Peter's bail was set at $2,500.[21] In today's money that is $68,545.79. Peter was only a laborer and a farm hand. There was no way he could have that kind of money. The average person does not have that kind of money even now. They *really* didn't want him out of jail.

The article "Charged with Incest" stated that Peter Tonge, a resident of Snyderville, was arrested on January 25, 1888, and the charge was incest against his daughter Sarah Tonge.[22] He was taken to Park City and held there overnight until his hearing in front of the United States commissioner the next morning in Salt Lake City. He was taken from Park City to Salt Lake on the train.

---

18 Gary Kimball, "Life Under China Bridge and Other Stories of Minorities in Old Park City" (Park City, Utah: Tramway Books, 2013).

19 "Bipolar Disorder Defined," Mayo Clinic database, (https://www.mayoclinic.org/diseases-conditions/bipolar-disorder: Accessed 27 Dec 2020) Definition below. "Bipolar disorder, formerly called manic depression, is a mental health condition that causes extreme mood swings that include emotional highs (mania or hypomania) and lows (depression). When you become depressed, you may feel sad or hopeless and lose interest or pleasure in most activities. When your mood shifts to mania or hypomania (less extreme than mania), you may feel euphoric, full of energy, or unusually irritable. These mood swings can affect sleep, energy, activity, judgment, behavior and the ability to think clearly. Episodes of mood swings may occur rarely or multiple times a year. While most people will experience some emotional symptoms between episodes, some may not experience any. Although bipolar disorder is a lifelong condition, you can manage your mood swings and other symptoms by following a treatment plan. In most cases, bipolar disorder is treated with medications and psychological counseling (psychotherapy)."

20 Ancestry, Find A Grave, database with images (http://www.findagrave.com: accessed 29 June 2019), memorial 68240313, Elizabeth Barnes Tonge (1845-1883), Heber City Cemetery, Heber City, Wasatch County, Utah, USA; gravestone photographed by (Living) Hammock.

21 My Heritage. "Committed To Jail," In Utah Newspapers, 1850-2003, images, My Heritage database, (http://www.myheritage.com: Accessed 07 August 2023) Peter Tonge, The Deseret News (Salt Lake City, UT) 20 January 1888, Vol XXI, Page 3.

22 My Heritage. "Charged with Incest," "In Utah Newspapers, 1850-2003," images, My Heritage database, (http://www.myheritage.com: Accessed 07 August 2023) Peter Tonge, The Deseret News (Salt Lake City, UT) 25 January 1888, Page 4.

Park City Museum

The jail where he was held in Park City still exists today. "The Dungeon," as it is called, is last remaining jail of the Utah Territorial Prison System. I have visited this jail a few times.

It is in Old Town Park City on Main Street and close to the post office. It is in the basement of the Park City Museum on Main Street.[23] The museum has a blue storefront, but the rest of it is red brick. The left half of the building has a couple of tall metal garage doors and a second store that has three large windows. This part of the building was once a fire station. In fact, there was a vintage red fire truck in the building as part of an exhibit.

The article "Marshall Dyer's Letter" from October 27, 1888, stated that Sarah M. Tonge was in jail with a babe on the charge of fortification.[24]

The article "Other Business" from March 8, 1888, stated Sarah Tong was arraigned for fortification and pleaded not guilty.[25]

The article "The Tonge Case" from April 25, 1888, stated that the child of the girl died in the morning, and Peter and Sarah Tonge's court appearance was to be postponed for a few days so that the family could bury the child.[26]

The newspaper article "A Revolting Affair" stated that Peter found Sarah with her deformed baby in Snyderville, Utah, the night he was arrested.[27]

---

23 Park City History, "Picture of the Park City Museum on Main Street." Image Online, (https://parkcityhistory.org/ Accessed: 30 May 2023.)

24 My Heritage. "Marshall Dyer's Letter," "In Chronicling America: Historic American Newspapers, 1791-1963," images, My Heritage database, (http://www.myheritage.com: Accessed 07 August 2023) Peter Tonge, The Salt Lake Herald (Salt Lake City, UT) 27 October 1888, Page 8.

25 My Heritage. "Other Business," "In Chronicling America: Historic American Newspapers, 1791-1963," images, My Heritage database, (http://www.myheritage.com: Accessed 07 August 2023) Sarah Tonge, The Salt Lake Herald (Salt Lake City, UT) 3 March 1888, Page 5.

26 My Heritage. "The Tonge Case," "In Chronicling America: Historic American Newspapers, 1791-1963," images, My Heritage database, (http://www.myheritage.com: Accessed 07 August 2023) Peter Tonge, The Salt Lake Herald (Salt Lake City, UT) 25 April 1888, Page 8.

27 Newspapers, "A Revolting Affair," images, Newspaper database, (http://www.newspaper.com: accessed 26 May 2019), Sarah and Peter

Transcript:

A REVOLTING AFFAIR

Peter Tonge Arrested on a Charge of Having Had Incestuous Relations With His Daughter – The Preliminary Examination? A Sure Case Made out Against the Brute. What the Neighbors Say.

Last Tuesday evening, U.S. Deputy Marshals Arthur Pratt, A.G. Dyer and I.A. Franks drove out from Salt Lake to arrest one Peter Tonge, a Snyderville wood chopper, on a most serious charge. Arriving in Snyderville, they proceeded to ascertain the whereabouts of Tonge. The deputies soon returned that their victim had fled and on following up his footsteps toward Park City were successful in finding him. Just below town, the officers met a man walking down the Utah Evanston grade and, suspecting him to be the man they wanted, hailed him, and he reluctantly came over to the sleigh, when he gave his name as William Moffat and at the request of the deputies got in the sleigh with them. They then drove over to Swetfield's house and in the meantime the prisoner admitted that his true name was Peter Tonge. Just as Deputy Dyer alighted? and started to search the house for Tonge's missing daughter, whom he has grossly offended. The man in custody acknowledged to the officers that she was there, that he had been lying when he told them she had gone to Evanston on a visit.

It now transpired that Tonge got wind of the officers coming after him and he walked with his daughter to Swetfield's house for the purpose of getting her out the way and arranging for his own escape. However, Miss Tonge was in too delicate a condition to be moved, but all the witnesses had in the meantime been subpoenaed. Tonge (Peter) was locked up for the night in the city jail and on Wednesday afternoon his preliminary examination was had before U.S. Commissioner Joe M. Cohen.

THE PRELIMINARY EXAMINATION

The defendant was arraigned before the Commissioner and the complaint which charges Tonge with having committed the crime of incest in that he on the 1st day of June 1887 unlawfully feloniously rudely and lasciviously cohabited with one Sarah Tonge then and there well-knowing the said person to be his daughter, etc., was read to him. He had no counsel, but pledged not guilty to the charge.

The best witness was Mrs. Sarah Head? a neighbor of the Tonges, and her evidence was mainly to the effect that Sarah

Tonge is the daughter of the defendant, that Sarah Tonge was not married, that she was encer te? (eccentric?) and that she did not accuse her father of the crime.

DON'T KNOW AND DON'T CARE

Nancy Tonge, the seventeen-year-old daughter of the defendant, swore that her unmarried sister Sarah was about twenty-three years old, that she was pregnant but did not know who the father of the coming child, never had raked her, and had no desire to be informed. Wim Barnes, her uncle, she said was supposed to have been the father of the first child born in Heber City, about two years age and which died. On further questioning, this model witness swore that there was but one bedroom with two beds in their house and that all the family occupied the one sleeping apartment, that she never had suspicions of incestuous relations existing between her father and sister, that her sister never kept company with any man, that she (Nancy) came home the last time to take care of the motherless children while her sister (Sarah) went to Evanston on a visit.

Mrs. Alice Meeks' testimony developed nothing new except that all the neighbors charged the crime on the father as was the case when the last illegitimate child was born in Heber City.

MORE DAMAGING EVIDENCE

John R. Elred also of Snyderville told of the many suspicions of the neighbors which implicated the old man.

John Swetfield swore that the defendant came to his house (the place where the girl gave birth to the deformed child, the secret, one late Wednesday night), had asked if his daughter be allowed to stay there till morning when he said she was going to Evanston on a visit.

Deputy Pratt made a statement about arresting Tonge and his equivocal talk while under arrest.

TONGES QUIBBLING

The defendant protested his innocence and in a mild way declared his daughter told him a young man with whom she got acquainted last spring was responsible in a paternal sense for the offspring. He said he used to sing in the Heber City choir and had never been cut off the Mormon church, though he was not now in good standing in it. His wife died four years ago, leaving a young child.

The Commissioner thought there was probable cause and held the arrogant brute in $2,500 bonds to wait the act on the grand jury and, failing to obtain suites, was taken down to the Pen. Sarah, his daughter, was placed the deputies that she would tell the truth and it is generally believed that her testimony the old fossil will be convicted. Under the Edmunds Tucker Law is from three 'o fifteen years imprisonment—none too much for the inhuman wretch.

The Edmunds-Tucker Law[28] "disincorporated both the LDS Church and the Perpetual Emigration Fund on the grounds that they fostered polygamy. The act prohibited the practice of polygamy and punished it with a fine of from $500 to $800 and imprisonment of up to five years. It dissolved the corporation of the church and directed the confiscation by the federal government of all church properties valued over a limit of $50,000.

The act was enforced by the U.S. Marshal and a host of deputies." The act of incest also falls under the Edmund–Tucker Law.

Peter's "William Moffat" alias is still being investigated; Peter may have just pulled it out of thin air, or he might have used it somewhere else before. He was a hardworking man and widower. He still had young children at home to take care of. Peter had only one thought when he found out there was a warrant out for his and Sarah's arrest, and that was to protect his wild daughter in any way he could.

Sarah's two babies were two more ancestors of mine that no one wanted to talk about. Those two innocent babies deserved to have the world know that they existed. It's almost like they have died repeatedly because people refused to talk about them. They were forgotten, but now they have been found. No one deserves to be forgotten. We are all human. We all matter.

With the bail amounts, it seems like they wanted to make an example of this father-and-daughter duo. This court case was sadder and more complicated than it appeared at first glance. All the twists and turns to it make it even more intriguing. Every new lead prompted new questions and more threads to pull to find the truth.

---

28 Wikipedia, " Edmunds–Tucker Act," database with images, Wikipedia, (https://en.wikipedia.org/wiki/Edmunds%e2%80%93Tucker_Act Accessed: 14 June 2024).

5 The Search Continues

My friend—the one who suggested looking for a court case—and I went back up to the Family History Library to do more research. We had narrowed down the time frame of when Sarah Tonge's path must have crossed Mr. Rose's. She had to have met him in prison because Maude, my great-grandmother, was born at the beginning of December 1888. That means Maude was conceived in prison. Apparently, this is embarrassing to some of my extended family. To me, it is history. It just enriches the story of my great-grandmother.

The poor, deformed baby was born at the end of January 1888 and died at the end of April.[29] That gives about two months where Maude could have been conceived. During those months, Sarah was still in prison, where she could have met Mr. Rose.

This poor baby is on my mind a lot. I am a little bit perturbed that all I have found out about this child was that they only called him or her "the baby," "the child," or "it." No name or gender have been found.

This baby was alive for about three months and was loved by at least Sarah and Peter Tonge. The baby must have had a name. The court even held off the trials a couple days so that the Tonge family could bury the child.[30]

No records of this child's burial have been found yet. There was a potter's cemetery at the penitentiary, but I have not been able to find the burial records for it yet.[31] The search will continue for this baby's burial site.

Utah Territorial Penitentiary Sugar House, 1855-1951

I feel it deep in my bones that Mr. Rose was the father of the deformed baby. There has been no physical proof of this, just a gut feeling. The Utah Territorial Penitentiary was only an adobe building and did not have very tall walls. Prisoners could have escaped, and they did frequently, according to the prisoner roster microfilm.[32]

Sarah Tonge and Mr. Rose could have met up somewhere for a rendezvous very easily before Mr. Rose had to be back at the penitentiary.

We started to look for Mr. Rose's name associated with the Utah Territorial Penitentiary in the year 1888. We spent a whole Saturday at the Family History Library searching for him.

---

29 My Heritage. "The Tonge Case," "In Chronicling America: Historic American Newspapers, 1791-1963," images, My Heritage database, (http://www.myheritage.com: Accessed 07 August 2023) Peter Tonge, The Salt Lake Herald (Salt Lake City, UT) 25 April 1888, Page 8.

30 My Heritage. "The Tonge Case," "In Chronicling America: Historic American Newspapers, 1791-1963," images, My Heritage database, (http://www.myheritage.com: Accessed 07 August 2023) Peter Tonge, The Salt Lake Herald (Salt Lake City, UT) 25 April 1888, Page 8.

31 Unknown, "Utah Territorial Prison, Sugar House, 1855-1951," Utah Railroads, Utah Rails (https://utahrails.net/utahrails/utah-territorial-prison.php: 2017) Accessed: 07 August 2023.

32 Utah State Archives. "Prison Commitment Registers," Utah State Archives, Salt Lake City, Salt Lake, Utah, USA, (http://www.archives.utah.org : accessed 12 June 2019), Microfilm: Reel 2 of series 80388, Prison Commitment Registers.

We did find a National Archive microfilm that had a list of prisoners for the Utah Territorial Penitentiary for 1888.[33] At the very top of the list were Sarah and Peter Tonge and what they were charged with—incest.

There were church records of the Church of Jesus Christ of Latter-day Saints found for Sarah Tonge Sabey and James Sabey in Wallsburg, Wasatch County, Utah, on a microfilm.[34] This supports their marriage license that states they lived in Wallsburg, Utah.[35]

A bunch of church records from the Church of Jesus Christ of Latter-day Saints for the Spratleys in American Fork were found this same day.[36] There were a lot of Spratleys in American Fork during the late 1800s. Without a given name, however, I could not narrow down who Jay Sabey's biological father was.

My friend Nicole, who is the same friend who suggested there may be court cases for the incest reference I found on the Church of Jesus Christ of Latter-day Saints church records, suggested we try to find out more about Sarah and Peter's court cases by going to the Utah State Archives in Salt Lake City.

Once upon a time, Nicole worked for an attorney as a paralegal and a research assistant. She loves researching everything.

She now owns her own business helping people figure out their water rights and land records. This all has to do with who owned what when and who is the rightful owner now.

All to do with history, really.

We did a bunch of research on their website, and there are a lot of microfilms that we still need to go through at the state archives. My friend also mentioned some journals in the University of Utah's Special Collections Library about the Utah Territorial Penitentiary and the prisons there.

---

33 FamilySearch, Family History Library, the Church of Jesus Christ of Latter-Day Saints, "National Archives Utah Penitentiary Report, 1888," images, Family History Library (FHL, Salt Lake City: accessed 25 May 2019) Peter and Sarah Tonge on Utah Penitentiary Report, National Archives Microfilm #: 1,602,239, last half of the film.

34 FamilySearch: Family History Library, the Church of Jesus Christ of Latter-Day Saints, "Record of members, 1876-1934; annual genealogical report, Form E, 1907-1948", United States & Canada 2nd Floor Film, 164612, Item 1 Film number 9072124, (Accessed 25 May 2019.) Entry for Sarah and James Sabey.

35 FamilySearch, "Utah, Marriages 1887-1940," images,", FamilySearch, (http://www.familysearch.org: accessed 4 April 2020,) Marriage License of James Sabey and Sarah Tonge, (1 October 1897), Microfilm#: 004579394, page 200, photocopy in the possession of the preparer (2020).

36 FamilySearch: Family History Library, the Church of Jesus Christ of Latter-Day Saints, "Early LDS Church Records – 1889, American Fork, Utah United States & Canada 2nd Floor Film, Film number: 025557, (Accessed 25 May 2019.) Entries for Spratley.

(The Daily Tribune.)

Utah penitentiary report, 1888.

Names of prisoners.	District.	Crime.	Sentence.	Date confined.	When discharged.— Remarks.
Tonge, Peter	3	Incest		Jan. 19, 1888	April 27, 1888, by court.
Tonge, Sarah	3	…do		Jan. 31, 1888	do.
Bargstrom, C. M.	1	Unlawful cohabitation.	4 months, $100, and cost.	Feb. 13, 1888	June 25, by court.
Anderson, C. A.	1	…do	2 months	…do	April 3, by commissioner.
Williams, Wm.	1	…do	6 months, $100, and cost.	…do	Aug. 13, 1888, by commissioner.
Crockett, Alvin	1	…do	4 months and cost	…do	May 24, 1888, paid cost.
Hansen, Hans P.	1	…do	6 months, $200, and cost.	…do	July 13, paid fine and cost.
Christianson, M.	1	Adultery	8 months	…do	Sept. 3, copper-act.
Merrill, M. W.	1	Unlawful cohabitation.	5 months and cost.	…do	June 18, paid fine and cost.
Hansen, James	1	…do	6 months, $100, and cost.	…do	Aug. 13, by commissioner.
Allen, Ira	1	…do	6 months, $300, and cost.	…do	July 13, paid fine and cost.
Griffin, William	1	Unlawful cohabitation and polygamy.	3½ years, $300, and cost.	…do	
Stauffen, Ulrich	1	Unlawful cohabitation.	6 months and cost	…do	July 13, paid cost.
Johnson, John*	3	…do	6 months, $150, and cost.	Feb. 24, 1888	
Cox, Edward	3	…do	6 months, $50, and cost.	Feb. 27, 1888	July 27, paid fine and cost.
Johnson, Alaus	3	…do	do	Feb. 29, 1888	Aug. 29, by commissioner.
Schuttler, B. H.	3	…do	6 months, $300, and cost.	…do	May 2, 1888, pardoned by Cleveland.
Sorensen, S. N.	1	…do	4 months, $50, and cost.	…do	June 9, paid fine and cost.
Thorpe, C. L.	1	…do	4 months, $100, and cost.	…do	June 12, paid fine and cost.
Pierpont, Thomas	3	…do	6 months, $300, and cost.	Mar. 1, 1888	Aug. 1, 1888, paid fine and cost.
Allred, Samuel	1	…do	6 months and cost.	Mar. 6, 1888	Aug. 6, paid cost.
Allred, Wm. M	1	…do	6 months, $100, and cost.	…do	Sept. 6, by commissioner.

Jubilee Haddessa

6 The J. Willard Marriott Library

I tried to schedule an appointment with the University of Utah's J. Willard Marriott Library – Special Collections Library for weeks via email. Many emails were sent, and no replies were ever received. Calling them several times had the same result, and several voicemail messages were left. No return phone calls ever came. So, it was time for an in-person visit. Sometimes, to get any response at all, you need to talk to a person face-to-face. I decided to take a Saturday and see how far I would get if the librarians had to deal with me in person.

The J. Willard Marriott Library is a five-story building. The Special Collections Library is on the fourth floor, and only a small part of the floor is open to patrons. You come up the stairs in the middle of the fourth floor and take a left through the atrium, then arrive at a large wooden reception desk. There are a few computers for patrons to log on to the library system to the right of the large reception desk. A patron reading room behind the reception desk is closed off with double glass doors. The receptionist would let patrons in by pushing a button and then pointing patrons through metal detectors before they entered the reading room.

My goal was to find everything on the Utah Territorial Penitentiary, from judge's papers and warden paper's to prisoner's journals and whatever else was to be found. I figured all the prisoners could do was serve time and write in journals. It is called "serving time" for a reason.

Hours were spent researching in the patron reading room. Several wooden tables filled the room, and each visitor could only check out one box, folder, or book of records at a time. Nothing could be photocopied, but I could take photos of documents using a cellphone or a digital camera. I discovered the journal of Ruger Clawson, a prisoner charged with polygamy.[37] This charge is sometimes called unlawful cohabitation.

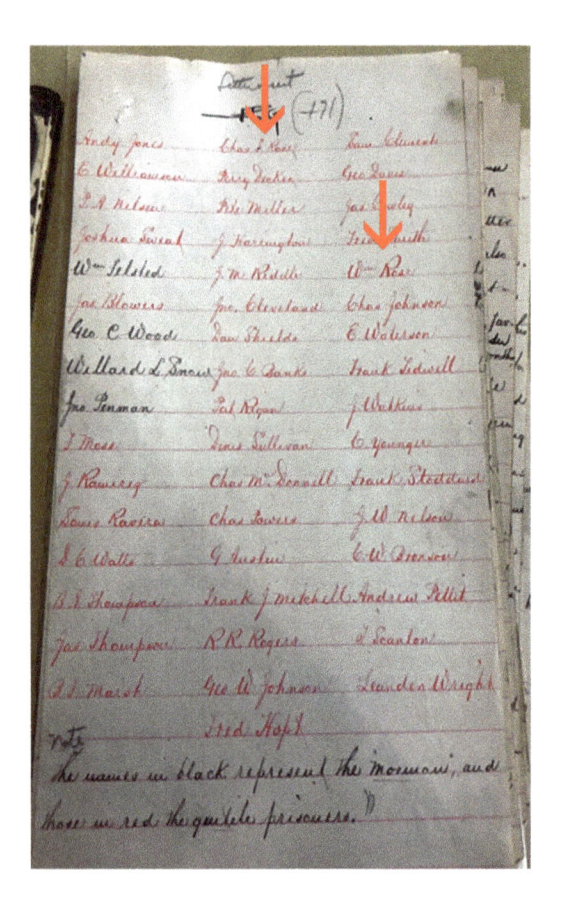

In Rudger's journal, he made a list of the prisoners who had been locked up with him. He wrote the names of members of The Church of Jesus Christ of Latter-day Saints in black ink and the names of the prisoners who were not members in red ink.

There were two names of interest for me: Charles F. Rose and Wm. Rose. Both were written in red ink, which meant neither of them were members of the Church of Jesus Christ of Latter-day Saints. At least, now I had a clue to Mr. Rose's given name. It was either Charles F. Rose or Wm Rose. Now, I had given names that I could narrow down which Mr. Rose was my Mr. Rose.

---

37 University of Utah, "Rudger Clawson Papers "Personal Experiences in the Utah State. Pen. Chronographs, (1886)", Images, University of Utah: J. Willard Marriott Library, Special Collections Library, (http://www.lib.utah.edu: accessed 15 May 2019), Charles F. Rose, Page 151-192, MS481 Box 2 Folder 5, Page 171.

34

7 Investigating At the Utah State Archives

My friend later took part of a day off from work to do some research for me at the state archives. That day, she found the grand jury minutes from the Tonge cases.

Reading the information on microfilm sometimes requires inverting the image to clearly make it out. Instead of viewing the film regularly with black writing on a white background, it will be white writing on a black background. Otherwise, some microfilms would be impossible to read due to the lightness of the ink. That is why some of the following excerpts from microfilm are white writing on a black background.

Jubilee Haddessa

Transcript:

The Grand Jury now come into court and through their Foreman present Thirteen (13) indited unto Findree? (unsure of wording) of which are pressed under the law of the United States and one of which is pressed under the laws of Utah Territory. Each is addressed a Trice Bill by the Foreman of the Grand Jury and each are filed in open court in the presence of the Grand Jury Trial.[38]

Against Peter Stevens; For assault attempted Rape; Bail Set at $800

Against Harry Hagreen; For making false witness of Paul Martin; Bail Set at $1,000

Against Harry Hagreen; For making false witness of Paul Martin; Bail set at $1,000

Against George B. Leonard; For making false witness of Paul Martin; Bail set at $1,000

Against George B. Leonard; For making false witness of Paul Martin; Bail set at $1,000

Against George B. Leonard; For making false witness of Paul Martin; Bail set at $1,000

Against George B. Leonard; For making false witness of Paul Martin; Bail set at $1,000

Against William J. Jinkins; For Unlawful Cohabitation; Bail set at $1,000

Against Peter Tong; For Incest; Bail set at $1,000

Against Lizzie Orr; For Fornication; Bail set at $500

Against Harrison Swine?; For Adultery; Bail set at $1,000

Against Sarah Tong; For Fornication; Bail set at $500

Against William Beedanger; For Adultery; Bail set at $500

And the Grand Jury makes written reports indicating the condition and the capacity of the Penitentiary. Also they find report of the commission trial -aeter (unsure of wording) also a report of the Ogden Executioner and which Indictment and Insured? Upon writing of George S. Peters U.S. Attorney. Their orders of Utah Warrants of Arrest is received by the clerk in each and all of the cases above are recorded and the Grand Jury anntipated? their cunios? (unsure of wording) and are Discharged by the court.

I find it fascinating that Peter Tonge was charged with incest, knowingly having sex with a relative, but Sarah Tonge was charged with fornication, having sex outside of marriage. These are two very different charges. Incest was a horrible crime, and still is. In the late 1800s, incest could be punished by three to fifteen years in the penitentiary under the Edmunds-Tucker Law.[39]

Today, it is a third-degree felony punishable by up to five years in prison and a $5,000 fine, according to the Utah state criminal code.[40]

The charge of fornication also fell under the Edmunds-Tucker Law in the late 1800s. Section 5 read, "That if an unmarried man or woman commits fornication, each of them shall be punished by imprisonment not exceeding six months, or by a fine not exceeding one hundred dollars."[41] This was a misdemeanor.

The charge of fornication was only removed from the Utah state laws in the last few years.[42] It was surprising to me that it took until 2019 for this to happen.

The Grand Jury minutes from Peter Tong's court case are as follows:

---

38 Utah State Archives and Records Service, "Territorial Third District Court, Grand Jury Minute Books, Series 1635." (First Accessed in 7 June 2019, Accessed again on 15 July 2024) 1888, Entries for Peter Tong and Sarah Tong.

39 Utah State Archives, "The Compiled Laws of Utah, The Declaration of Independence and Constitution of the United States and Statues of the United States Locally Applicable and Important:, Compiled and Published, By Authority Vol I, Salt Lake City, Utah, Herbert Pembroke, Book, Job and Legal Blank Printer, 72 East Temple Street, 1888. Page 115, Section 4. Incest.

40 Wikipedia, "Legality of incest in the United States", database, Wikipedia, (https://en.wikipedia.org/wiki/Legality_of_incest_in_the_United_States Accessed: 14 June 2024) Utah.

41 Utah States Archives, "The Compiled Laws of Utah, The Declaration of Independence and Constitution of the United States and Statues of the United States Locally Applicable and Important", Compiled and Published, By Authority Vol I, Salt Lake City, Utah, Herbert Pembroke, Book, Job and Legal Blank Printer, 72 East Temple Street, 1888. Page 115 -116, Section 5. Fornication.

42 NPR, National, Sasha Ingber, "Utah Repeals 1973 Law That Criminalized Sex Outside Of Marriage," (https://www.npr.org/2019/03/29/708042810/utah-repeals-1973-law-that-criminalized-sex-outside-of-marriage Accessed: 14 June 2024) 29 March 2019.

Unraveling the Family Secret

Transcript:

United States of America Vs. Peter Tong[43]
Incest

This cause now coming regularly for trial with H.S. Winter appearing for the Defendant, the trial here is began and the following named jury are trusted good and lawful men are duly impartial and sworn to try this incest trial: Jethro

---

43 Utah State Archives and Records Service, "Territorial Third District Court, Grand Jury Minute Books, Series 1635." (First Accessed in 7 June 2019, Accessed again on 15 July 2024) 1888, Entry for Peter Tong.

Rydalch, James Binebett, W.F. Clinton, E.P. Shepherd, S.C. Pancake, Fred W. Tracy, W.F. Hudsen, William Vanderhart, William Jenson John Sunphry?, Edward Pickering, Edward Mullay, wherein the indictment is sealed and the defendant's plea of Not Guilty is stated to the Jury by the clerk, wherein Maggie Tong, E.A. Frank, John Swetfield are duly sworn and testify for the prosecution and Peter Ivin, Sarah Tong, and Peter Tong are duly sworn and examined for the defense wherein the case is argued by H.S. Winter for defendant and the Court instructs the jury and the jury writers in charge of a sworn officer of the Court to consider of their indict and subsequently the jury return into the Court and they said verdict trial, "Us the jurors empaneled in the above case find the defendant guilty as charged in the indictment.

Dated April 26th A.D. 1888

F. R. Jones Foreman

Wherein the jury are discharged from further consideration of the court and upon motion of the defendant Attorney, it is ordered that the defendant have thirty (30) days from this day in which to prepare and file a Bill of Exception herein.

The Bill of Exception must have been filed because in the court case of Peter Tong, he was actually found not guilty of incest. The Bill of Exception will need to be found to continue this line of inquiry.

The following Grand Jury minutes are from Sarah Tong's court case:

Transcript:

United States of America Vs. Sarah Tong[44]
Fornication

In appearing from the indictment of the of the U.S. Attorney that a connection accused? be had in this case. Upon motion of U.S. Attorney, it is that this cause and this same be dismissed and the defendant be discharged from custody and go home without? day.

She also found Sarah and Peter Tonge on the Utah Territorial Penitentiary Prisoner Roster.[45]

Transcript:

Name of Prisoner: Peter Tong
Crime: Incest
Date of Conviction: 19th January 1888
Occupation: Laborer
Weight: 115
Complexion: Florid
Age: 45
Height: 5' 5"
Color of Eyes: Gray
Color of Hair: Light Brown
Other Distinctive Markers: England; temperate; can't read or write; widowed
Remarks: Discharged By 3rd District Court 27th April 1888 Acquitted.

Name of Prisoner: Sarah Tong
On What Account Held: Come Coher Park City 3rd District Court
Crime: Incest Indited 24th February 1888 for Fornication Pleaded to the charge Not Guilty. 2nd March 1888
Date of Conviction: 31st January 1888
Occupation: Domestic
Weight: 120
Complexion: Medium Dark
Age: 23
Height: 5' ½"
Color of Eyes: Blue
Color of Hair: Light Brown
Other Distinctive Markers: England; unmarried; can read and write; temperate
Remarks: Discharge By 3rd District Court 27th April 1888 Acquitted

This microfilm has a lot of useful information on it. I love this film.

It is a treasure trove that I am still studying to this day.

There are also about ten more prisoner rosters I will eventually need to get my hands on.

---

44 Utah State Archives and Records Service, "Territorial Third District Court, Grand Jury Minute Books, Series 1635." (First Accessed in 7 June 2019, Accessed again on 15 July 2024) 1888, Entry for Sarah Tong.

45 Utah State Archives. "Prison Commitment Registers," Utah State Archives, Salt Lake City, Salt Lake, Utah, USA, (http://www.archives.utah.org : accessed 12 June 2019), Peter Tonge on Prison Roster, (1888), Microfilm: Reel 2 of series 80388, Prison Commitment Registers, On Slide 442, page 139, 3rd book. Utah State Archive. "Prison Commitment Registers," Images, Utah State Archives, Salt Lake City, Salt Lake, Utah, USA, (http://www.archives.utah.org : accessed 12 June 2019), Sarah Tonge on Prison Roster, (1888), Microfilm: Reel 2 of series 80388, Prison Commitment Registers, On Slide 442, page 139, 3rd book.

Unraveling the Family Secret

> United States of America) Fornication.
>   vs.   ) It appearing from the statement of the U.S.
> Sarah Young   ) Attorney that a conviction cannot be had in
> this cause, upon motion of U.S. Attorney, it is ordered that this cause
> is and the same is hereby dismissed and that defendant be discharged
> from custody and go hence without day.

Jubilee Haddessa

The Utah State Archives will send you whole microfilms digitized on Google Drive. I sent an inquiry to the Utah State Archives staff for the first microfilm of the prisoner roster to be sent to me through email. The cost for them to digitize a microfilm was $40, but I did not have to pay because someone before me had already done so. This microfilm was sent to my email for free; that was another miracle.

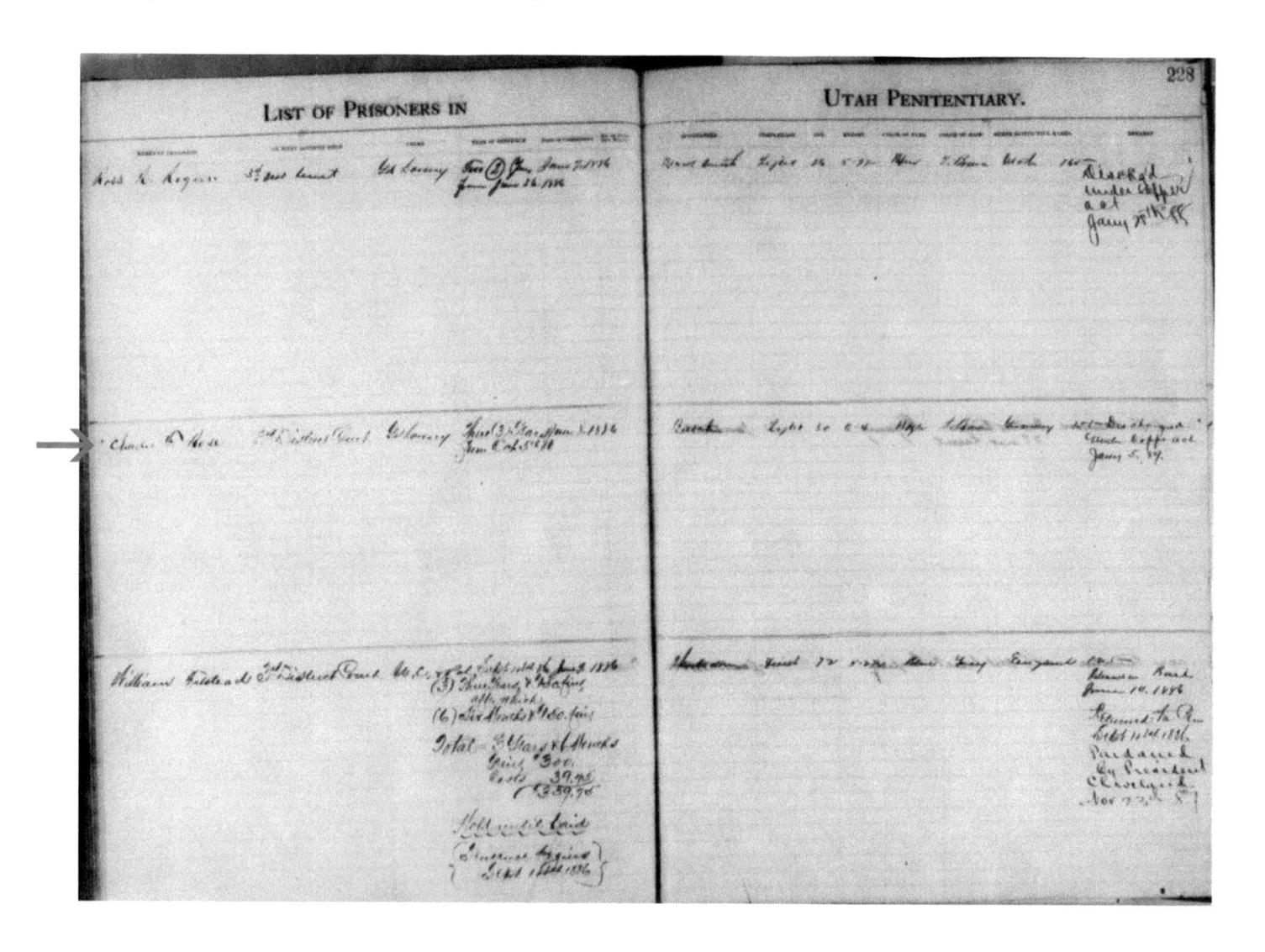

An Unexpected Discovery!

Receiving this microfilm of the Utah Territorial Penitentiary prisoner roster was so exciting, and I was naughty.

I had to start looking at the film on my phone at work using the Google Drive app, slide by slide.

It was almost like a compulsion had taken over me; I had to start looking at the microfilm, no matter where I was or what I was doing.

It was a small miracle that I wasn't caught. It was fascinating to read every single slide. It was a snapshot of all these people's lives on what was probably their worst day.

Transcript:
Name of Prisoner: Charles F Rose
On What Account Held: 3rd District Court
Crime: Grand Larceny
Term sentence: June 8, 1886
Occupation: Butcher
Weight: 155
Complexion: Light
Age: 30
Height: 5' 4"
Color of Eyes: Hazel
Color of Hair: Light Brown
Other Distinctive Markers: Germany
Remarks: Discharged under Copper Act January 25th, 1889

I put the phone down to help a guest. When I picked my phone back up a few minutes later, my thumb slipped and the microfilm skipped forward a few dozen slides or more. Then, it froze on a slide that had a Charles F. Rose on it.[46] He had been indicted by the Third District Court in August of 1886 on the charge of grand larceny. He was sentenced to three and a half years in the penitentiary. Charles's complexion was ruddy (having a healthy red color, rosy cheeks), and he had brown hair and brown eyes.

He was thirty in 1886. This gave me an estimated birth year of 1856. I knew he had to be around Sarah's age, give or take a few years. Sarah was in her mid-twenties around this time. He was released from prison in January 1889—approximately one month after my great-grandmother was born in Evanston, Wyoming in December 1888. Evanston, Wyoming is where Sarah Tonge went after she was released from prison in April 1888 to lick her wounds.

This means that between the months that Sarah spent in prison and the time she was released, February and April 1888, Maude was conceived in prison. This makes sense because during the late 1800s, the penitentiary was overcrowded. The men were in the main part of the prison and the women stayed with the warden and his family. His house was on the prison grounds, so men and women could mingle unsupervised if they were careful.

The thing that excited me the most about the entry I found on the microfilm for Charles F. Rose, was that the "Additional Notes" section listed his home country as Germany. Remember: On the 1900 census, all I knew about Mr. Rose was that his surname was Rose and that he was from Germany. I also knew that he had to have connections to Evanston, Wyoming, because that was where my great-grandmother was born.

When I saw Germany as his home country, I got all warm from head to toe. A tingling feeling, really, a burning in my bosom. It was confirmation from God that I had finally found my biological second-great-grandfather. The man I had been seeking for ten long years had finally been found.

This was not the end of the story, though. I knew there was so much more information I needed to find, such as how he came to the United States, who his parents were, and more.

At that very moment, I was elated. I wanted to jump up and down and scream in excitement. So many thoughts were running through me. I was thankfully able to contain myself and finish work. As soon as I was outside the building after work, I was back to jumping for joy. I called my friend who helped with the research and told her what I had found.

"How do you know that this is him, your second-great-grandfather?" she asked.

I told her about the warm feeling and just knowing, as if he was speaking to me from beyond the grave. Plus, he was released from jail a month after Maude was born.

My friend said she would do some research in the newspapers about Charles F. Rose. A day later, she had found a newspaper article from the Park Record, the Park City newspaper, called "Rose, the Thief."[47]

Transcript:

ROSE, THE THIEF
He is captured at Evanston, jumps the train and is now in Deputies care (?)

Last Sunday morning Henry Newell went to his stable to saddle his horse when he missed the saddle and the bridle. Inquiry developed the Charles F. Rose had taken them. Rose is a fellow who was employed by Mr. Newell until about two months ago, and ... that time had been butchering in Snyderville. On Sunday John B.? Allen missed his horse, which had been grazing the ill back of the Cresent concentrator, and a little detective work convinced Misters Newell and Allan that Rose had stolen the horse also. Rose told some friends a few days ago that he intended to go to Wyoming, and to others he said he was going to move to Salt Lake. Accordingly, a descriptive telegram was sent to Evanston with orders to arrest the culprit.

---

46 Utah State Archives, "Prison Commitment Registers," Utah State Archives, Salt Lake City, Salt Lake, Utah, USA, (http://www.archives.utah.org : accessed 12 June 2019), Charles F. Rose on Prison Roster, (1886), Microfilm: Reel 2 of series 80388, Prison Commitment Registers, On Slide 260, page 233, 1st book.

47 University of Utah. "Rose, the Thief," images, Newspapers.lib.utah Database, (https://www.newspapers.lib.utah.edu: accessed 13 June 2019,) Park Record (Park City, Summit, Utah, USA), 05 Jun 1886, page 3.

ROSE, THE THIEF.

He is Captured at Evanston, Jumps the Train and is Now in Durance Vile.

Last Sunday morning Henry Newell went to his stable to saddle his horse, when he missed the saddle and bridle. Inquiry developed the fact that Charles F. Rose had taken them. Rose is a fellow who was employed by Mr. Newell until about two months ago, and since that time has been butchering in Snydervile. On Sunday John V. Allen missed his horse which had been grazing on the hill back of the Crescent concentrator, and a little detective work convinced Messrs. Newell and Allen that Rose had stolen the horse also. Rose had told some friends a few days ago that he intended to go to Wyoming, and to others he said he was going to move to Salt Lake. Accordingly a descriptive telegram was sent to Evanston with orders to arrest the culprit.

HE IS ARRESTED.

Tuesday morning Rose was confronted by the sheriff of Evanston and his deputy and ordered to surrender. Rose drew his gun on the officer, and had it not been for the deputy's prompt action a bloody struggle would have ensued. Deputy Sheriff M. J. Gerraty and Henry Newell left on Wednesday morning's train for Evanston and returned in the evening with the prisoner. The sheriff of Evanston took the prisoner to the state line where he was immediately re-arrested by Deputy Gerraty. Rose was closely watched on the train and he was very docile until near Atkin on a ranch, a few miles below Evanston, when he asked leave to get a drink of water which was granted, he not being handcuffed. When near the door he bounded out, and from the platform jumped to the ground, a distance of several feet as the train was going at full speed. Deputy Gerraty was at his heels and tried to grab him back but failed and fired his pistol at him.

THE GETAWAY DODGE

Was, for a time, thought by the officers and the excited passengers on the train to be a fatal one. The train was finally stopped and backed up to the place where Rose was seen to roll down the embankment. He was just recovering his senses but had managed to crawl under a pile of ties. He was fished out and afterwards landed in the city jail. Rose was severely bruised and felt quite sore about the head and chest. It was a risky break and a very close call.

THE EXAMINATION.

Rose was taken before Justice James Thursday morning to answer to the charge of petty larceny in stealing the saddle and bridle. To this he pleaded guilty, and in default of $200 bonds was remanded to the custody of the deputy sheriff pending the action of the grand jury in the case.

At 11 o'clock Thursday morning U. S. Commissioner Cupit began an examination of the charge of grand larceny in stealing the horse. Henry Newell, John T. Allen and M. J. Gerraty testified for the prosecution, when an adjournment was taken to 2 o'clock.

B. V. Martin appeared as counsel for the defendant Rose, who plead not

sheriff pending the action of the grand jury in the case. At 11 o'clock Thursday morning, U.S. Commissioner Cepit began an examination of the charge of grand larceny in stealing the horse. Henry Newell, John F. Allen and M.J. Gerrety testified for the prosecution. When adjournment was taken to 2 o'clock, H.V. Martin appeared as counsel for the defendant Rose, who pled not guilty to the charge of grand larceny.

After a brief talk by the attorneys, and in the affidavit, assistant Allison, the rather preliminary examination of the case was continued till Monday at 10 o'clock am. Rose again failed to secure bondman and was locked up in a cell. The saddle and bridle were recovered by Mr. Newell, and the horse arrived here today, There is no doubt but that Rose will be convicted of the misdemeanor and will serve a term in the Pen.

HE IS ARRESTED
Tuesday morning, Rose was confronted by the sheriff of Evanston and his deputy and ordered to surrender. Rose drew his gun on the officer, and had it not been for the deputy's prompt action, a bloody struggle would have ensured. Deputy Sheriff F. Gerraty and Henry Newell left on the Wednesday morning train for Evanston and returned in the evening with the Prisoner. The Sheriff of Evanston took the prisoner to the state line, where he was immediately arrested by Deputy Gerraty. Rose was closely watched on the train, and he was very docile until near Atkinson's? ranch, a few miles of low ground, when he asked leave to get a drink of water, which was granted, he detoured handcuffed to the door. When near the door, he bounded out, and from the platform jumped to the ground, a distance of several feet as the train was going full speed. Deputy Gerraty was at his back and tried to grab him back, but failed and raise his pistol at him.

THE GEO + CALVARY MODE
Was, for a time, absorbed by the officers and the express passengers on the train to be a fatal case. The train was eventually backed up to the place where Rose was seen to roll down the embankment. He was just regaining his senses, but had managed to crawl under a pile of ties. He was severely bruised and felt quite sore about the head and chest. It was a lucky break and a very close call.

THE EXAMINATION
Rose was taken before Justice James Thursday morning to answer to the charge of petty larceny in stealing the saddle and bridles. To this he pleaded guilty, and in default of $300 bonds was returned to the custody of the deputy

The article talks about how Charles F. Rose stole a horse and bridle to go to Evanston to meet up with some friends. He was also a resident of Snyderville, Utah. The crazy thing was that this was 1886, two years before Sarah and Peter Tonge ended up in prison. This article helped to prove my theory that Mr. Rose had connections to Utah and Evanston. Charles reminds me so much of my younger brother—living life and flying by the seat of his pants.

I told two of my friends about the Tonges and Charles. I mentioned it was weird that a butcher would steal a horse. One of my friends disagreed. "Well, in the late 1800s when beef was scarce, they would eat all sorts of different kinds of meat," he said. "Horse meat was just one of those types of meat that was regularly available. Beef was quite scarce." This actually made a lot of sense in my head. I had some knowledge of this way back in the recesses of my mind.

At least Charles wasn't in Texas when he stole that horse. In Texas, stealing a horse was a capital offense. He would have been hanged on the spot if this crime had been committed in the Lone Star State.

I told my mother about my latest discoveries. She was thrilled that I had found my biological second-great-grandfather. She assured me that my research was sound, but also cautioned that it sounded like I had my work cut out for me.

My mom had changed her mind about Peter Tonge because of the evidence that I had compiled. The trail had gotten hot, but this was just the beginning of the journey. This investigation has now turned into a lifelong quest, a quest that keeps leading me to the Utah Territorial Prison System like a magnet.

8 More Leads

My friend Nicole came across a court case for Charles F. Rose at the Utah State Archives. I had to figure out a weekday I could take off to go to Salt Lake City and find it. My sister happened to be coming to visit from Arizona in mid-June, a few short weeks after the discovery, and needed someone to pick her up at the Salt Lake City International Airport.

In the meantime, Nicole and I found more newspaper articles—snippets, really, such as the theft of a horse from a former employer[48]—about Charles's case. I also had time to interview my ailing father, who had been in a lockdown memory rest home for about ten years at that point.[49]

On June 19, 2019, my mom and I asked him about the following questions. Keep in mind that my dad had dementia at the time. So, any answers I got out of him, I took with a grain of salt.

What do you remember about your grandmother, Maude? She liked to cook. She liked to garden. She was very diligent and a hard worker. She had red hair.

What do you know about Sarah Tonge? Nothing

What do you know about Peter Tonge? Nothing

Do you know how James Sabey and Sarah Tonge meet? James Sabey was looking for a nanny to watch his children and Sarah applied for the job. She was watching his children as well as her own and they fell in love.

Do you know who got all of Maude's personal effects? No

Did Roy Sabey have children? No idea

Did Jay Sabey have special needs? Mom says that he was. Dad doesn't remember.

What do you remember about your Grandfather John? Very hard worker all the time. My uncle told us he would steal John's hat when he was younger and ran around the house and had John chase him. He feels bad about it now, realizing that John was blind, but he also thinks that John was having the time of his life, too.

How far did you get on the 1900 census about Maude and Roy's biological father with the last name of Rose? Or Jay's biological father with the last name of Spratley? We didn't get very far. My wife was the one who found that 1900 census. That's as far as we got.

Tell me more about raising sheep. Grandma and Grandpa would live off of about two hundred to two hundred and fifty dollars a month from the Bureau of Land Management. Traded things like milk for things they needed. Cutting grain and beef and hauling rock stick out in my mind.

What was life like at the sheep camps? Dad remembers traveling to the desert out by Jericho. They would herd the sheep down Provo Canyon by horses and sheep. They did sheep for about thirty years or more. They had dairy cows before sheep and always had a little bit of beef cows until about 2007 when Dad sold his part of the farm. Dad taught me how to milk a cow when I was very young, and I can remember sheep at a very young age, too. They had to milk the dairy cows two times a day, morning and night. Forest in the summer. Desert in the summer. Big Glade in the summers. The troughs up by Big Glade were put there by the forest rangers. Mom says they sold the dairy cows about 1963, right before Dad when on his mission. They sold the sheep about 1960.

What do you remember about the Tonges? Not much

Were the Tonges a frustrating family line to work on? Yes

---

48 University of Utah. "Rose, the Thief," images, Newspapers.lib.utah Database, (https://www.newspapers.lib.utah.edu: accessed 13 June 2019,) Park Record (Park City, Summit, Utah, USA), 05 Jun 1886, page 3.

49 Private. Grand Son of Maude Rose Sabey Thompson, Vinyard, Utah County, Utah, USA. Interviewed by Private, 19 June 2019. Transcript (handwritten). Privately held by interviewer. Heber City, Wasatch, Utah, USA, 2019.

What do you remember about doing family history? One day, my mom found seven lines in a book at the Family History Library in Salt Lake. I remember having stacks of microfilms and being told to find a certain name. I did find some.

Did you keep a research journal? The Book of Remembrance

Tell me about some of your experiences at the Family History Center in Salt Lake City. John waited for Maud to grow up. He really liked her red hair. He had asked James Sabey for her hand in marriage, and he said yes.

I told my dad about finding Charles F. Rose. I thought it would be the best Father's Day gift ever. I do not know how much he understood about what I was telling him due to his Alzheimer's disease. His memory was sketchy, but I knew I had to tell him I had found Charles before he passed away. My dad had been trying to find him for a long time. I hope something from what I told him sunk in.

I also filled my sister in. She was quite impressed and thanked me for telling her. She said that the incest cases I had proved wrong were just history and anyone trying to stop me from doing the research would have to explain to God why they were trying to stop me. It is all history! Like me, she does not understand why people want to stop the past from coming to light.

I even conducted a phone interview with one of my dad's cousins, the only one who I really got along with. She was willing to listen to me explain my research, never judging me like other members of my dad's extended family did. The first question she had was, "How did you find his last name?"[50]

In telling her the story, she became open to letting me interview her about what she knew about the Tonges and Charles F. Rose. I recorded it in my journal. Below is the transcript:

June 20, 2019

I had the most interesting conversation with one of my dad's cousins last night. We talked for almost an hour and a half. I was so excited to tell her about the story of how I found Charles F. Rose. I told her everything and that I disproved of the incest thing.

She was very happy to hear that. She was told that Sarah had three children by Peter and that they had to chain Peter up to keep him away from Sarah. She always thought he was a monster and that there was a special circle in hell for him.

However, she is very relieved that I was able to disprove that. I have now changed two people's minds about Peter.

She told me that they knew that Maude was conceived in prison, but that it was a redheaded jailer, not a prisoner. She knew my story rang true from the moment I left the voicemail on her phone two nights ago. She said that Dad's side of the family were mostly embarrassed by Sarah and Peter and the whole thought about having a grandmother that had been conceived in prison.

She had been researching on and off about this for years, but she has not found anything. She now knows it had to be me. That I am doing the Lord's will. That this all needs to come out, that the Utah Territorial Prison prisoners all have their stories told, and that their work also needs to be done. The Lord is going to use me in so many ways for his own purposes. This is going to be huge.

She also told me that Maude liked those who toed the line and didn't get along with those who were rowdy or wild.

She said that Sarah met James Sabey by being a domestic helper in his house in Lehi, Utah. She did his cleaning, cooking, and laundry. This was added to what Dad told me about Sarah babysitting James's children. I did not know that James Sabey even lived in Lehi.

How did they end up in Wallsburg then?

Where was the Sabey homestead in Wallsburg?

She says that James's other children from previous marriages hated Sarah, Maude, Roy and Jay, and they didn't want James to even associate with them. To this day, there is a Sabey family faction in Lehi and Provo area that will not associate or even acknowledge our side of the family even exists.

I told her that I think Sarah was bipolar, with her hypersexism and all the newspapers say she had an interesting temperament.

I also told her that I think one of my great-uncles had it because of all the stories that Grandpa and my dad had told me about him. She was like, "Do not tell me. I don't need to know. That uncle was my favorite uncle. I do not need that ruined for me." Done deal. He was my favorite great-uncle, too.

I also explained that my dad, her cousin, had recently been

---

50 Sabey, (Living). Grand Daughter of Maude Rose Sabey Thompson, Orem, Utah, Utah, USA. Interviewed by (Living) Thompson, 11 April 2020. Transcript (was a phone call). Privately held by interviewer. Heber City, Wasatch, Utah, USA, 2020.

diagnosed with bipolar disorder and Alzheimer's, and that bipolarism can be hereditary, the same with Alzheimer's. She told me that I was right to think Sarah had bipolarism. That rang true in her mind as soon as I told her.

She was like, "Well, that explains a few things."

She also warned me about which relatives to talk to about this and which not.

And she wants me to update her every week on the developments I have. And she will be praying for me and the Rose line and be putting my name in the temple every two weeks.

She is so excited that I am finding the truth and not letting anyone stop me.

I told her that I had asked her sister about the 1900 census and the fact that Maude's last name on it was Rose. Her sister had shut me down and said that Maude's father was James Sabey and to leave it alone.

She was like, "Well, that's not very nice."

I was like, "All I wanted to do was learn about the Rose and the Spratley lines. We are responsible for learning about them, too."

She was like, "This whole thing embarrasses my sister and most of my older cousins, but that is no excuse not to find our ancestors."

It was a wonderful conversation. She said she has been searching for these people as well on and off on her own, but couldn't find anything.

This whole new revelation makes me so angry and so sad all at once. My dad's cousins all knew that Sarah and Peter were both in prison for a time. In addition, they KNEW that Maude was conceived in prison. And that her father was a "redheaded jailer." They never knew Mr. Rose's or Mr. Spratley's first names, but they were on the trail and completely jumped off the path. I mean . . . they KNEW and did nothing about it.

You are accountable for what you know. They knew and did nothing about it. I just cannot get my head wrapped around that. They were trying to hide people who existed; this, to me, was like they killed them all over again. No one deserves to be forgotten.

She also believed I was on the right track and told me to feel free to bounce things off her when I needed to. I asked her where Sarah and Peter Tonge were buried.

She said that Sarah Tonge Sabey was buried in the Provo Pioneer Cemetery.[51] She said that she would show me where Sarah was buried one day. She told me that she had no idea where Peter Tonge was buried. She didn't think anyone actually knew where Peter Tonge was buried. No one ever talked about what had happened to Peter Tonge. It's like no one wanted to know.

That last part really made me angry. It's like no one even wanted to acknowledge that Peter ever existed. It only spurred me on to find where he was buried, to find out more about what had happened to him.

I decided to look up Peter Tonge and Elizabeth Barnes Tonge on Billiongraves.com and Findagrave.com, and I got lucky with Findagrave.com. Their grave marker was in the Heber City Cemetery, Heber City, Utah.[52] It floored me that my paternal third-great-grandparents were buried in Wasatch County, and no one had even really cared to look for their burial site. The incest issue may have played a large role in this. It makes me sad, mad, and disappointed all at once.

My friend, Nicole and I decided to find the gravesite in person, via GPS.

It was a very rainy and windy evening. It took us a little bit to find it, but when we did, I started to cry. I felt like Peter was very happy that I was there, that I was finding the truth about him, and that it hadn't stopped me. No one wanted to talk about this family line for decades. The fact that taboo topics, personal judgements, and rumors still haunted the Tonges even to this day left me furious. Still, a light was slowly being shone on this bit of history.

On the right of Peter and Elizabeth's gravestone were about five graves from the family of William Barnes, Elizabeth's brother.

One gravestone—shaped like a tree stump—belonged to sixteen-year-old Robert Barnes, who died

---

51 Ancestry, Find A Grave, database with images (http://www.findagrave.com: accessed 29 June 2019), memorial 40230543, Sarah Tonge Sabey (1865-1939), Provo City Pioneer Cemetery, Provo, Utah, Utah, USA; gravestone photographed by Twin of an Angel.

52 Ancestry, Find A Grave, database with images (http://www.findagrave.com: accessed 29 June 2019), memorial 68240313, Elizabeth Barnes Tonge (1845-1883), Heber City Cemetery, Heber City, Wasatch County, Utah, USA; gravestone photographed by (Living) Hammock. Ancestry, Find A Grave, database with images (http://www.findagrave.com: accessed 20 June 2019), memorial 68240369, Peter Tonge (1842-1920), Heber City Cemetery, Heber City, Wasatch County, Utah, USA; gravestone photographed by (Living) Hammock.

Headstone of Peter Tonge and his wife, Elizabeth Barnes Tonge

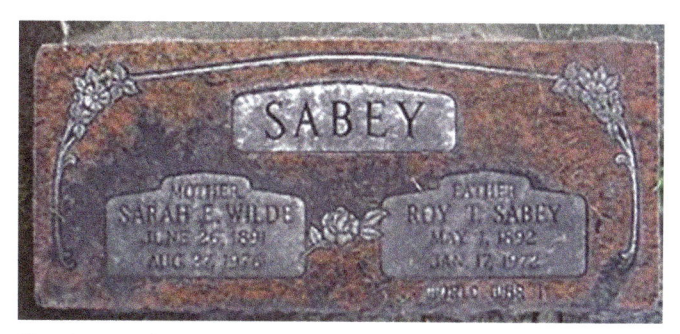

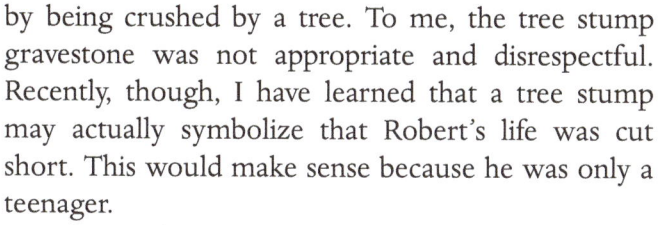

Headstone of Roy T. Sabey and his wife, Sarah E. Wilde Sabey

Headstone of Sarah Tonge Sabey

Headstone of Jay Spratley Sabey

by being crushed by a tree. To me, the tree stump gravestone was not appropriate and disrespectful. Recently, though, I have learned that a tree stump may actually symbolize that Robert's life was cut short. This would make sense because he was only a teenager.

As for Sarah Tonge's resting place, my dad's cousin and I tried unsuccessfully for months to get our schedules to coordinate to go see the grave together. So, one day after researching in Salt Lake City, I decided to take the long way home through Provo. My goal was to see if I could find Sarah's resting place for myself.

When I finally made my way to the Provo Pioneer Cemetery, I knew that I had to find the cemetery office to see whether they had records of who was buried in the cemetery. There was a three-inch-thick black binder in a wooden box on the office's porch. The wooden box was to protect the binder from the elements.

Inside the binder were all the names of the people who were buried there and which plots they were buried in.

The binder was organized alphabetically by last name, which made the search so much easier. There were only three Sabeys buried in the cemetery: Sarah Sabey, Roy Sabey, and Jay Sabey.[53]

What an unexpected discovery! Sarah's two eldest sons were buried there as well—and on either side of their mother in the same plot.

---

53 Ancestry, Find A Grave, database with images (http://www.findagrave.com: accessed 22 April 2021), memorial 40661721, Roy Sabey (1892-

By taking a picture of their page in the binder and comparing the information to the large cemetery map plastered on a wooden billboard next to the office, I figured out where Plot 12 and Row 3 were located.

It was really a miracle that out of thousands of people buried in the Provo Cemetery, there were only three Sabeys. The graves were within walking distance, but I drove there instead. The plot is right on a corner of the road. After parking my car, I started walking the plot, row by row, until I found Sarah and her sons' gravestones. They are under a beautiful shade tree.

Roy T. Sabey and his wife Sarah E. Wilde are buried on the left side of Sarah.[54] This is how I found out that Roy had been married. Roy's gravestone also had World War I engraved on it, which meant that he fought in World War I. That told me I needed to find records of his time spent in the military.

Sarah Tonge Sabey was buried between her two sons.[55]

Jay Sabey was buried on the right side of his mother.[56]

As I stood at the resting place of my second-great-grandmother, I couldn't help but cry. Emotionally, I was totally overwhelmed. Sarah was proud of me. I could feel in my bones that she was comforting me and encouraging me to go on. That was the day I knew I had to write her story down and share it with the world, no matter what opposition I faced. Someone, somewhere will be touched by Sarah's story, and it will help them find the courage to go on. That is what her story did for me and what it continues to do for me. It sustains me and has given me strength when I felt I could no longer go on.

1972), Provo City Cemetery, Provo, Utah, Utah, USA; gravestone photographed by Twin of an Angel. Ancestry, Find A Grave, database with images (http://www.findagrave.com: accessed 1 May 2021), memorial 40661795, Jay Sabey (1896-1933), Provo City Cemetery, Provo, Utah, Utah, USA; gravestone photographed by Twin of an Angel.

54 Ancestry, Find A Grave, database with images (http://www.findagrave.com: accessed 22 April 2021), memorial 40661721, Roy Sabey (1892-1972), Provo City Cemetery, Provo, Utah, Utah, USA; gravestone photographed by Twin of an Angel.

55 Ancestry, Find A Grave, database with images (http://www.findagrave.com: accessed 29 June 2019), memorial 40230543, Sarah Tonge Sabey (1865-1939), Provo City Pioneer Cemetery, Provo, Utah, Utah, USA; gravestone photographed by Twin of an Angel.

56 Ancestry, Find A Grave, database with images (http://www.findagrave.com: accessed 1 May 2021), memorial 40661795, Jay Sabey (1896-1933), Provo City Cemetery, Provo, Utah, Utah, USA; gravestone photographed by Twin of an Angel.

9 Tracing the Tonge Family's Timeline

When I arrived home from the Provo Pioneer Cemetery, I immediately headed to Familysearch.org and Ancestry.com to narrow down a timeline of the Tonges' arrival in the United States of America from England. Another reason to research this timeline was to figure out when the Tonges settled in Evanston.

The reason that the Tonges ended up in Evanston, according to what I found, was because William Barnes joined the Church of Jesus Christ of Latter-day Saints in England, along with Elizabeth and her family. William Barnes, Richard Barnes, and Alice Howarth, Richard's wife, traveled to the United States before the Tonges came over in 1873.

The trio traveled in the pioneer wagon company of Daniel Thompson from July 24, 1866, through Sept 28, 1866, from Wyoming, Nebraska, to Salt Lake City, Utah.[57] The document stated that the relationship between William and Richard Barnes was unclear. On the 1880 census, William's son Robert Barnes was listed as born in Evanston, Wyoming, and four years old.[58] Robert was born in the year 1876.

Peter and Elizabeth's daughter Margaret Alice Tonge was born in Evanston in 1876 as well.[59] This means that the Tonge family and William Barnes's family were both living in Evanston in that year.

The reason for William Barnes being in Evanston in 1876 is still unclear. He might have been on a mission from Brigham Young to help settle Evanston, though no proof of this has been found yet.

Both the Tonges and Barneses were in Heber City, Utah, on the 1880 United States census.[60] They must have moved to Utah about the same time.

Research for the Tonge family in England before 1873 revealed that Peter Tonge's family appeared on the 1871 England and Wales Census in Farnworth, Lancashire, England, United Kingdom.[61]

---

57 Family Search. "Utah Mormon Pioneer Overland Travel Database, 1847-1868," database with images, FamilySearch (https://familysearch.org/ark:/61903/1:1:QK9B-CBCQ : Accessed 28 April 2024), William Henry Barnes, 29 Sep 1866; from "Mormon Pioneer Overland Travel: 1847-1868," database, > The Church of Jesus Christ of Latter-day Saints (https://history.lds.org/overlandtravels/ : 2004-).

58 Family Search. "United States Census, 1880", database with images, FamilySearch (https://www.familysearch.org/ark:/61903/1:1:MNSL-5ZY : Accessed 28 April 2024), Entry for William Barnes and Margrette. Barnes, 1880. Source: Person Number: 0, Source Household Id: 4252650, Source Sheet Number: 314, External Repository Name: The U.S. National Archives and Records Administration (NARA), New Household Flag: External Line Number: 00014, Source Sheet Letter: C, Source Volume: 1.

59 Family Search: Family History Library of the Church of Jesus Christ of Latter-Day Saints, "The Church of Jesus Christ of Latter-Day Saints Membership records, U.S.A. and Canada; Heber East Ward Records of Members Early 1902" images, Family History Library, (FHL, Salt Lake City, Utah: Accessed 11 May 2019), Church records of the Tonges, Libr. No. 13271, Microfilm Number 0026026, About Page 51.

60 Ancestry, "United States Census 1880," database, Ancestry, (https://Ancestry.com: accessed 11 May 2019, entry for Peter Tonge (b. 1842), Heber City, Wasatch, Utah, USA, dist. 090, sudist. Blank: p. 1, fam. 10; "affiliated film number" 1339.

61 FamilySearch International, "England and Wales Census, 1871," database, FamilySearch, (https:// https://www.familysearch.org/ark:/61903/3:1:939K-R32R-5: accessed 07 July 2019), entry for Peter Tonge (b. 1842), Farnworth, St. Johns, England, dist. St. Johns, sudist. Blank: p. 22, fam. 122; "affiliated film number" 004411418.

Jubilee Haddessa

Transcript:

Name: Peter Tonge
Sex: Male
Age: 27
Birth Year (Estimated): 1844
Birthplace: Bolton, Lancashire
Marital Status: Married
Occupation: Cotton Spinner
Relationship to Head of Household: Head
Relationship Code: Head
Event Type: Census
Event Date: 1871
Event Place: Farnworth, Lancashire, England, United Kingdom
Sub-District: Farnworth
Enumeration District: 10
Entry Number: 13

Peter Tonge's spouses and children:
Name: Elizabeth Tonge
Sex: Female
Age: 25
Birth Year (Estimated): 1846
Birthplace: Bolton, Lancashire
Marital Status: Married
Occupation: Cotton Piecer
Relationship to Head of Household: Wife
Relationship Code: Wife
Event Type: Census
Event Date: 1871
Event Place: Farnworth, Lancashire, England, United Kingdom
Sub-District: Farnworth
Enumeration District: 10
Entry Number: 14

Name: Sarah Tonge
Sex: Female
Age: 6
Birth Year (Estimated): 1865
Birthplace: Bolton, Lancashire
Marital Status: Unknown
Relationship to Head of Household: Daughter
Relationship Code: Daughter
Event Type: Census

Event Date: 1871
Event Place: Farnworth, Lancashire, England, United Kingdom
Sub-District: Farnworth
Enumeration District: 10
Entry Number: 17

Name: Mary E Tonge
Sex: Female
Age: 0
Birthplace: Farnworth, Lancashire
Relationship to Head of Household: Daughter
Relationship Code: Daughter
Event Type: Census
Event Date: 1871
Event Place: Farnworth, Lancashire, England, United Kingdom
Sub-District: Farnworth
Enumeration District: 10
Entry Number: 18

Other People on This Record:
Name: Edward Tonge
Sex: Male
Age: 18
Birth Year (Estimated): 1853
Birthplace: Bolton, Lancashire
Marital Status: Unknown
Occupation: Coal Miner
Relationship to Head of Household: Brother
Relationship Code: Brother
Event Type: Census
Event Date: 1871
Event Place: Farnworth, Lancashire, England, United Kingdom
Sub-District: Farnworth
Enumeration District: 10
Entry Number: 15

Name: Nancy Barnes
Sex: Female
Age: 52
Birth Year (Estimated): 1819
Birthplace: Bolton, Lancashire
Marital Status: Widowed
Occupation: Housekeeper
Relationship to Head of Household: Mother-in-law
Relationship Code: Mother-in-law
Event Type: Census

Event Date: 1871
Event Place: Farnworth, Lancashire, England, United Kingdom
Sub-District: Farnworth
Enumeration District: 10
Entry Number: 16

Name: Brigham Barnes
Sex: Male
Age: 15
Birth Year (Estimated): 1856
Birthplace: Bolton, Lancashire
Marital Status: Unknown
Occupation: Coal Miner
Relationship to Head of Household: Brother-in-law
Relationship Code: Brother-in-law
Event Type: Census
Event Date: 1871
Event Place: Farnworth, Lancashire, England, United Kingdom
Sub-District: Farnworth
Enumeration District: 10
Entry Number: 19

Peter Tonge was the head of the family, and his mother-in-law and brother-in-law were living with them. There was a remarkable discovery made while studying this document. Another daughter, Mary E. Tonge, was mentioned. She was only a baby. She was not mentioned on any other documentation that I had about the Tonge family. After double- and triple-checking all of the documents I had, I came to the conclusion that she must have died at a young age.

In 1880, ten years later, the Tonges welcomed another daughter with a very similar name, Mary Elizabeth Tonge. This follows the English tradition of naming a newborn after a child with the same name that died young. The first Mary E. Tonge must have passed away before the Tonges came over to the United States in 1873.

This Mary E. Tonge was the fourth person lost to history that I found while on this journey. The others were Sarah Tonge's two babies that died young and Charles F. Rose.

This Mary E. Tonge fell into my lap, and I was so excited to find her. I wasn't looking for her, but I found her nonetheless. My mom was so excited about this discovery, and she encouraged me to keep looking for answers.

10 More Leads Just From Living My Life

In the Summer of 2019, I received an email from FamilySearch informing me about the Tonge family's crossing from England to New York on the USS Wyoming in 1873.[62] The website where this passenger list was found was called Saints by Sea, which was hosted by Brigham Young University. I had been looking for this information for years.[63]

There had been a family story that the Tonges came over on the USS Wyoming passenger boat in 1873 with a bunch of other pioneers traveling to Salt Lake City from England, but I never could find the documents to back it up until this one. I was excited that FamilySearch found something for me that I had been missing.

USS Wyoming; 3 Sep 1873, from Liverpool Arrival, 19 Sep 1873 at New York; Church Leader John B. Fairbanks

---

[62] Brigham Young University, Provo, Utah, Utah, USA, "Saints by Sea, Latter-day Saint Immigration to America, U.S. Wyoming Passenger List, 1873," database with images, Saints by Sea, Latter-day Saint Immigration to America, (http://www.saintsbysea.lib.byu.edu: accessed 4 September 2021), Family of Peter Tonge, (1873), citing BMR, Book #1041, pp. 288-299 (FHL #025,692); Customs #1006 (FHL #175,738); SMR, 1873 (FHL #025,696).

[63] BYU, Saints By Sea, Photo of the U.S.S. Wyoming, (https://saintsbysea.lib.byu.edu/mii/voyage/493? Accessed: 8 June 2024.)

Transcript:

Last Name: *Tonge*
First Name: *Peter*
Age: *30*
Origin: *Bolton*
Tonge, Betsey (Age: 27)
Tonge, Mary (Age: infant)
Tonge, Sarah (Age: 7)

The rest of 2019 included many random finds and leads. They weren't necessarily leads on this family line, though. Leads came just by me living my life day to day. There were some very cool experiences that I will never forget.

Park City, Heber City, Midway, Provo, Orem, Salt Lake City and Evanston, along with the Utah Territorial Prison System, kept pulling me back for more research. Apparently, I needed to learn all that I could about those locations. My rule of thumb: You must know the history of a place to figure out why your ancestors settled there in the first place. To be a genealogist is to have a love of history *and* the people who lived it.

Some of the weirdest and wildest family history leads found me. In late August of 2019, I started working as a housekeeper at the Homestead Resort in Midway, Utah. I found out that a friend of mine that I hadn't seen in about two years was working there, too. We started cleaning rooms and doing other tasks together.

One day, we had an encounter with Fannie's ghost. Fannie was the founder and one-time owner of the Homestead. The resort was founded in 1886. We were cleaning rooms in the Bunk House, which was exactly what it sounds like. It was a red two-story building with about eight rooms containing bunk beds on each floor. It is one of three or four original buildings there that have survived since 1886.

The resort's founding was in the same time period as the Tonges and Charles F. Rose were around Wasatch County and Summit County. These locations were not that far from Midway—only about five to ten miles apart on a map. The fact that people in 1886 could go up and over the mountain, up Snake Creek and Guard's Men's Pass, to drop over into downtown Park City made me think that maybe the Tonges or Charles F. Rose had connections to the Homestead. They could have stayed at the Homestead Hotel—the Homestead Hotel was what it was called back in the late 1800s—at some point.

The hotel had to have some sort of records that kept track of the guests who have stayed at the hotel starting in 1886, or at least I hoped they did. I told my cleaning partner about this idea that popped into my head and asked her if she knew of any records or ledgers of guests that dated that far back.

She did not know of any such records or anyone who would know of them, but she noted that the home of the original owners (Fannie and Simon) still existed on the resort's land. There are rumors that the ghosts of Fannie, Simon, and their two sons still haunt the property of the Homestead Resort to this day.

Excitement filled my soul. "Cool! How do I get in there?"

"We can ask the front desk for the key to unlock it and go inside one day."

I filed that information away for later.

My friend and I were cleaning a room on the ground floor of the Barn, a red building at the resort, a couple of weeks later. This room was painted white and had two queen-sized beds against the right-hand wall. Its bathroom—with a vanity with a mirror and a sink, a bathtub-shower combination, and a toilet—was also all white. I was cleaning the bathroom while my friend was vacuuming the main room. My phone was on the nightstand between the two beds playing music because we cleaned faster when there was music on.

Out of nowhere, my phone shut off. I was in the bathroom with my head over the bathtub, and my friend was vacuuming on the other side of the bed. Neither of us were anywhere near my phone to turn it off. Also, it took about thirty seconds for someone to turn my phone off by holding down the Power button.

It seemed like there was another presence in the room, only unseen. Because it felt like a kind spirit, I thought nothing of it. I turned my phone back on, resumed the music, and went back to cleaning. A few minutes later, my friend and I were making one of the beds when my phone shut off out of nowhere again.

I was a bit frustrated and decided to speak to the spirit in the room. "Fannie, if you do not like the song that is playing on my phone, please do not turn it off again. You can just hit the Fast-forward button—the arrows pointing to the right—to skip the song. We are kind of on a time crunch right now, and I don't have time to keep turning on my phone over and over."

I turned the phone back on and went back to making the bed. The music skipped ahead in the middle of a song and went on to the next song. I only nodded, glad the ghost had listened. I then went to the bathroom to gather up my cleaning supplies so we could move on to the next room on our list.

"Fannie just skipped the song again," my friend called out.

"She probably didn't like it," I called back. "Maybe she wants our attention for some reason."

Between the two of us, we figured that Fannie wanted us to go check out her old home. We determined we had about twenty minutes to spare, so we went to the front desk to ask them for permission to go in Fannie's home.

"I don't care if you go in there or not," the front desk manager said. "It's your nightmare." Apparently, she feared the old home. She opened the door of the home for us, then decided to come with us at the last minute.

The front side of the two-story home is a beautiful blue. We entered through a side door; I did not get a picture of that entrance.[64]

The old home had been used to house guests at one time. There are these gorgeous, frosted glass numbered windows above each of the bedrooms.

---

64 Homestead Resort, Midway, Wasatch County, Utah, United States, Photos were taken by Jubilee Haddessa on 21 September 2019.

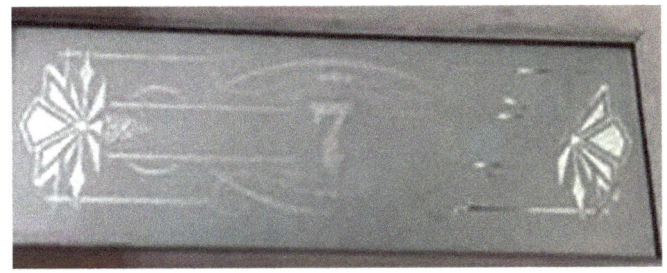

There were about ten bedrooms all together.

Beautiful brass and frosted glass chandeliers are prevalent in the home.

The staircase to the second floor was quite narrow. People could only go up and down one at a time. This was common in pioneer homes. On the wall to the right of the stairs was a picture frame with the name of the home and its history.

Transcript:

VIRGINIA HOUSE

So named because of the magnificent Virginia Creeper that entwines it. This property was originally homesteaded in 1875 by Samuel Thompson and was known as the "Hot Pots" because of the interesting hot water crater formations which abound in the area, the largest of which is located 200 feet north of this building. In 1878, Simon Schneitter purchased the property from Samuel Thompson and it soon became a great attraction to the people of the mining town of Park City who arrived in white top buggies and surreys. This interest inspired Mr. Schneitter to create a bathing resort, and in 1886 this two-story hotel was built with a large frame kitchen adjoining it to the south, where Mrs. Schneitter prepared and served family-style chicken dinners.

Jubilee Haddessa

Many prominent families, some nationally known, have enjoyed the serene atmosphere of this picturesque little hotel long before the advent of plumbing, and it was not until 1952 that the convenience of modern bathrooms found its way into this quiet old building. Many of the "heavenly beds" are collector's items, and as much of the old-fashioned furnishings have been retained as possible. Note the lovely old porch light overhead, originally made for kerosene and later converted to electricity.

This history gave me Simon and Fannie's last name, Schneitter.

Their last name was also on one of the frosted glass windows above a doorway: "The Schneitter Family Hotel."[65]

There were also some cool antiques in the home, however I was unable to find any records besides the Virginia House picture or the last name Schneitter of Fannie and Simon in the frosted glass. That was enough information to start researching Fannie and Simon Schneitter, though.

The tour of the old Virginia House was very helpful. Armed with the Schneitter name and the dates that they were in Midway, I sat down to do some research on the family. Billiongraves.com has them buried in Midway Cemetery in Midway.[66] Their headstone gave me their birthdates and death dates. After searching the Midway Cemetery for a few minutes, I located Simon and Fannie's gravesite.

Fannie was born September 10, 1874, and died September 1, 1950. Simon was born June 30, 1860, and died September 27, 1938. With this information, I looked up Fannie and Simon Schneitter on Familysearch.org.

Come to find out, I am related to Fannie on my maternal grandmother's side. She was my tenth cousin three times removed. I believe this is what Fannie was trying to tell me. I would never have found out my relation to her if I had stopped looking for Charles F. Rose.

I feel very honored to have found this information about Fannie.

Simon and Fannie Schneitter, husband and wife

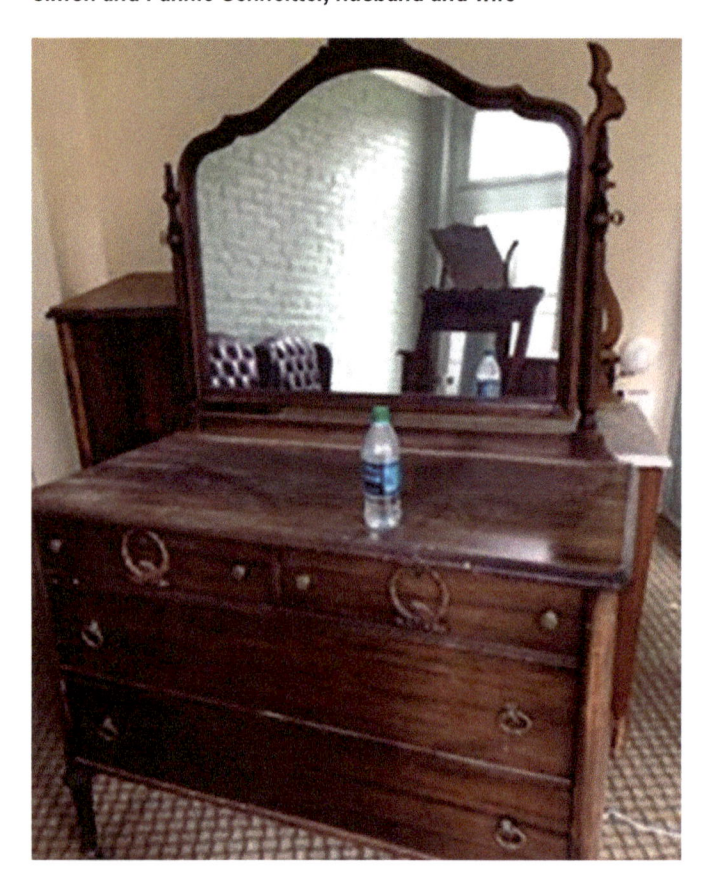

---

65 Homestead Resort, Midway, Wasatch County, Utah, United States, Photos were taken by Jubilee Haddessa on 21 September 2019.

66 Billion Graves, "Headstone of Simon and Fannie Schneitter," database with images, Billiongraves, (https://billiongraves.com/grave/Fannie-m-Schneitter/4453081 Accessed 22 September 2019), Midway City Cemetery, Midway, Wasatch County, Utah, United States, Entry for Simon and Fannie Schneitter

11 Court Case of Charles F. Rose

In mid-June 2019, I took off two days in the middle of the week to pick up my sister and her boys from Salt Lake City's airport. During that time, we stopped by the Utah State Archives for an hour or two so I could find the court case of Charles F. Rose.

The Utah State Archives' building, on Rio Grande Street not far from Temple Square and the Salt Palace, served as the main train depot in downtown Salt Lake City in the late 1800s. The building is so beautiful. It has vaulted ceilings, with a dome on one side of the building. Part of the building is not accessible to the public; that is where they keep all the records.

The main entrance opens into the domed room and includes an art gallery. A security guard held watch from behind a beautiful wooden reception desk on the left. He directed us to the left, toward the library/study room. Visitors must check in on a computer there before passing through the library's wooden gate and toward its tables, computers, and microfilm readers. On the library's outside walls were floor-to-ceiling wooden bookshelves, complete with a rolling ladder. There was also a large wooden desk where the archivists sat, ready to help. We found the court case of Charles F. Rose—all twenty-one pages—on a microfilm.[67]

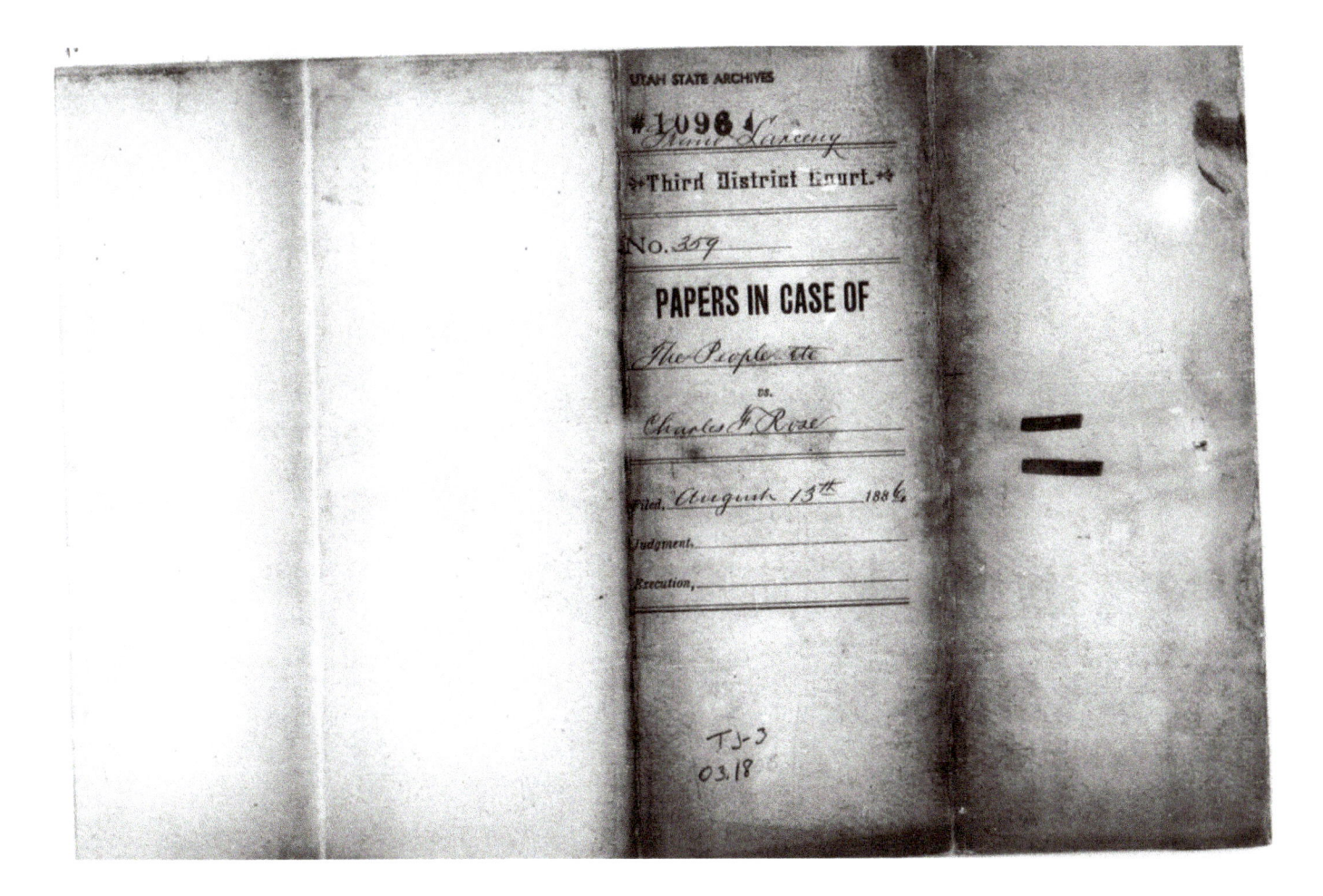

---

67 Utah State Archives. "Charles Rose's Court Case (1886)," Utah State Archives Library, Salt Lake City, Utah, USA, (http://www.archives.utah.org: accessed 22 June 2019), Court Case of Charles F. Rose, (1886), Microfilm #: 3, Series 6838, Case # 359, Certificate #: 1096.

Jubilee Haddessa

Transcript:

UTAH STATE ARCHIVES
#1096

Grand Larceny

Third District Court
No. 359
PAPERS IN CASE OF
The People Etc Vs. Charles F. Rose
Filed, August 13th, 1886
TJ-303.18

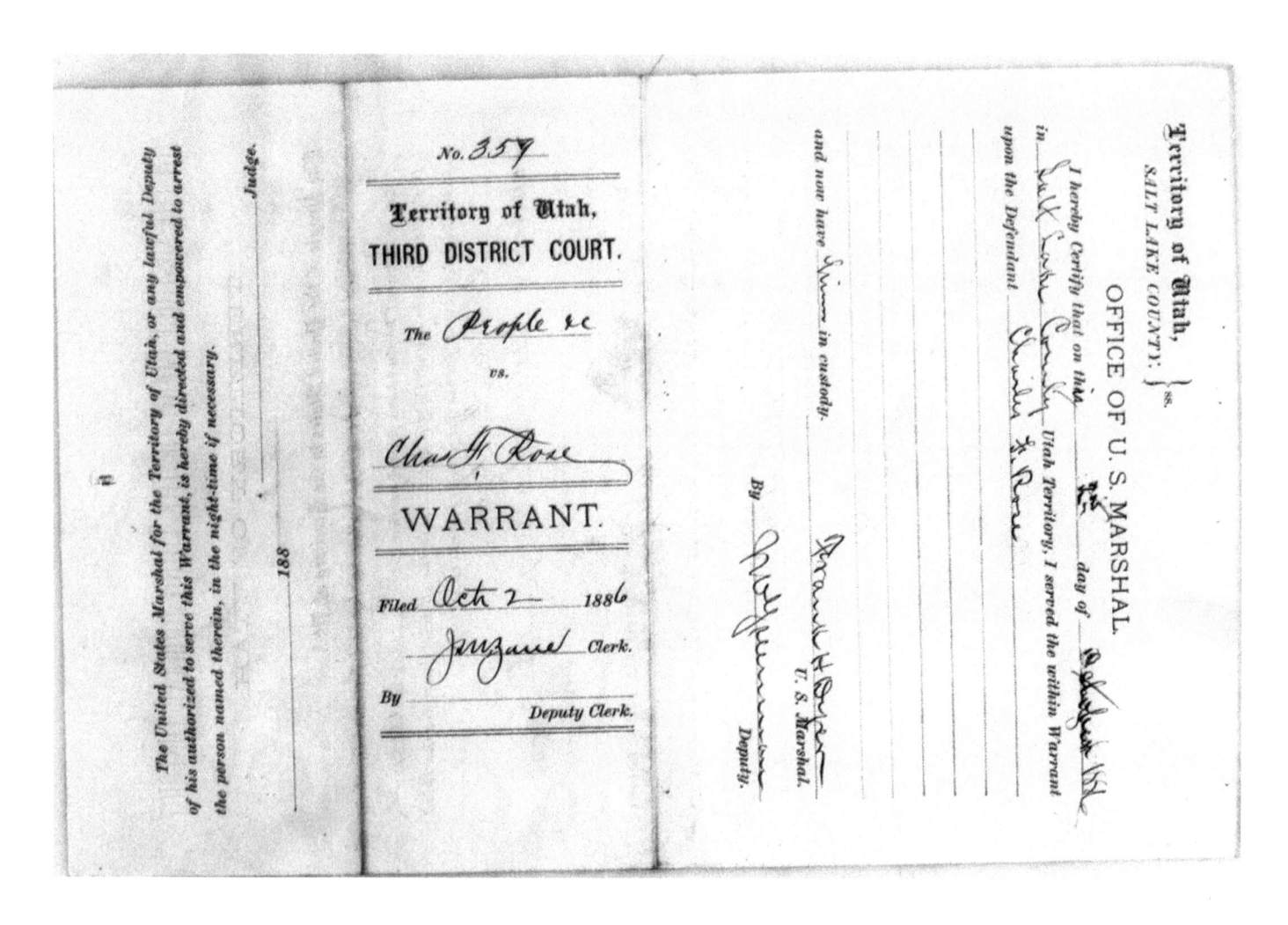

The United States Marshal for the Territory of Utah, or any lawful Deputy of his Authorized to serve this Warrant, is hereby directed and empowered to arrest the person named therein, in the night-time if necessary.

No. 359
Territory of Utah, Third District Court.
The People etc. Vs. Chas F. Rose
WARRANT Filed Oct 2, 1886
J. M. Zane, Clerk

Territory of Utah,
Salt Lake County,

OFFICE OF U.S. MARSHAL
    I hereby Certify that on this 2nd day of October 1886 in Salt Lake County Utah Territory, I served the Within Warrant upon the Defendant Charles F. Rose and now have him in custody.
Frank H. Dyer, U.S. Marshal
By NoYearman?, Deputy

IN THE DISTRICT COURT OF THE THIRD JUDICIAL DISTRICT

OF THE

TERRITORY OF UTAH.

The People of the United States in the Territory of Utah.

To the U. S. Marshal for said Territory, Greeting:

An Indictment having been found on the 13th day of August A. D. eighteen hundred and eighty-Six in the District Court for the Third Judicial District in and for the Territory of Utah, charging Charles F. Rose with the crime of Grand Larceny

You are therefore commanded to forthwith arrest the above named Charles F. Rose and bring him before that Court, to answer said indictment, or if the Court has adjourned for the term, that you keep, or cause him to be safely kept in custody until the further order of this Court; or if he require it, that you take him before Wm McKay U. S. Commissioner, to be admitted to bail in the sum of $500

C. S. Zane Judge.

WITNESS my hand and the seal of said Court, affixed at Salt Lake City, this 13th day of August A. D. 1886.

J. M. Zane Clerk.

By U. G. McMillan Deputy Clerk.

Territory of Utah, In the Third Judicial District Court, Utah

The people of the Territory of Utah

against

Charles F. Rose

Charles F. Rose is accused by the Grand Jury of this Court, by this indictment, of the crime of Grand Larceny committed as follows: the said Charles F. Rose on the 29th day of May A. D. eighteen hundred and eighty-six at the County of Summit in said Territory of Utah. one grey gelding of the age of four years of the property & chattels of one John F. Allen, they and there being, then & there did feloniously steal take and driveaway

contrary to the form of the statutes of said Territory in such case made and provided, and against the peace and dignity of the people aforesaid.

W. H. Dickson, U. S. Dist. Att'y.

Chas. A. Tewksbury, Foreman of Grand Jury.

IN THE DISTRICT COURT OF THE THIRD JUDICIAL DISTRICT OF THE TERRITORY OF UTAH

The people of the United States in the Territory of Utah.

To the U.S. Marshal for said Territory, Greeting:

An Indictment having been found on the 13th day of August A. D. eighteen hundred and eighty-six in the District Court for the Third Judicial District in and for the Territory of Utah, charging Charles F. Rose with the crime of Grand Larceny

You are therefore commanded to forthwith arrest the above named and bring him before the Court, to answer said indictment, or if the court has adjourned for the term, that you keep, or cause him to be safely kept in custody until the further order of this Court; of if he require it, that you take him before Wm McKay U.S. Commissioner, to be admitted to bail in the sum of $500.

C.S.S. Zane, Judge.

WITNESS my hand and the seal of said Court, affixed At Salt Lake City, this 13th day of August A.D. 1886.
J.M. Zane, Clerk
By N.G. McMillan, Deputy Clerk

TERRITORY OF UTAH, IN THE THIRD JUDICIAL DISTRICT COURT, UTAH

The people of the Territory of Utah Against Charles F. Rose

Charles F. Rose is accused by the Grand Jury of this Court, by this indictment, of the crime of Grand Larceny committed as follows: the said Charles F. Rose on the 29th day of May A.D. eighteen hundred and eighty-six at the County of Summit in said Territory of Utah. one grey gelding of the age of four years of the property & chattels of one John F. Allen. Then and there being, then and there did feloniously steal take and drive away. contrary to the form of the statutes of said Territory in such case made and provided, and against the peace and dignity of the people aforesaid.

W.H. Dickson, U.S. Dist. Att'y
Chas. A. Tewkesbury?, Foreman of Grand Jury.

TERRITORY OF UTAH, } ss. IN THE JUSTICE'S COURT,
County of Summit

Park City Precinct.

The People of the United States of the Territory of Utah:

To any Sheriff, Constable, Marshal or Policeman in the County of Summit Territory of Utah,

A COMPLAINT, upon oath, having been laid this day before me by Henry Newell that the crime of Grand Larceny by taking stealing leading and driving away one horse the property of John Allen has been committed, and accusing Charles Roe

thereof, you are thereof commanded forthwith to arrest the above named Charles Roe and bring him before me, forthwith, at my office in said precinct, in said County of Summit or, in case of my absence or inability to act, before the nearest or most accessible magistrate in this County.

Dated at my office, in said Precinct, in said County of Summit, this first day of June A. D. 1886.

Thomas Cupit
Justice of the Peace of said Precinct.

WARRANT OF ARREST.   Printed and for Sale at the SALT LAKE HERALD OFFICE.

Witnesses:
John F. Allen
Martin Gerraty

No. 359
DISTRICT COURT
The People of the Territory of Utah Vs. Chas. F. Rose
Indictment for Grand Larceny
A true Bill
Chas. A. Tewkesbury, Foreman of Grand Jury.
Presented in open Court, by the Foreman of the Grand Jury, in the presence of the Grand Jury, and filed by me, 13th day of August 1886
J.M. Zane, Clerk
N. G. McMillan, Deputy Clerk.
W. H. Dickson, U.S. Att'y
500

1886 Aug 13, Issued Warrant
1886 Oct 2. Arrgd pled Not Guilty
1886 Oct 5. Pled Guilty
1886 Oct 5. Sentenced Penitentiary 3 years.

TERRITORY OF UTAH, County of Summit
IN THE JUSTICE'S COURT, Park City Precinct.

The People of the United States of the Territory of Utah:
To any Sheriff, Constable, Marshal or Policeman in the county of Summit Territory of Utah,

A COMPLAINT, upon oath, having been laid this day before me by Henry Newell that the crime of Grand Larceny by taking stealing leading and driving away one horse the property of John Allen has been committed, and accusing Charles Rose
Thereof, you are thereof commanded forthwith to arrest the above named Charles Rose and bring him before me, forthwith, at my office in said precinct, in said County of Summit or, in case of my absence or inability to act, before the nearest of most accessible magistrate in the County.
  Dated at my office, in said Precinct, in said County of Summit, this First day of June A,D. 1886.
Thomas Cupit, Justice of the Peace of said Precinct.

Warrant of Arrest
Printed and for Sale at the SALT LAKE HERALD OFFICE.
The within Charles F. Rose, having been brought before me, under this Warrant, he is committed for examination to the Sheriff of the County of Summit Utah.
  Dated this 3rd day of June 1886.
Thomas Cupit, Justice of the Peace of said Precinct

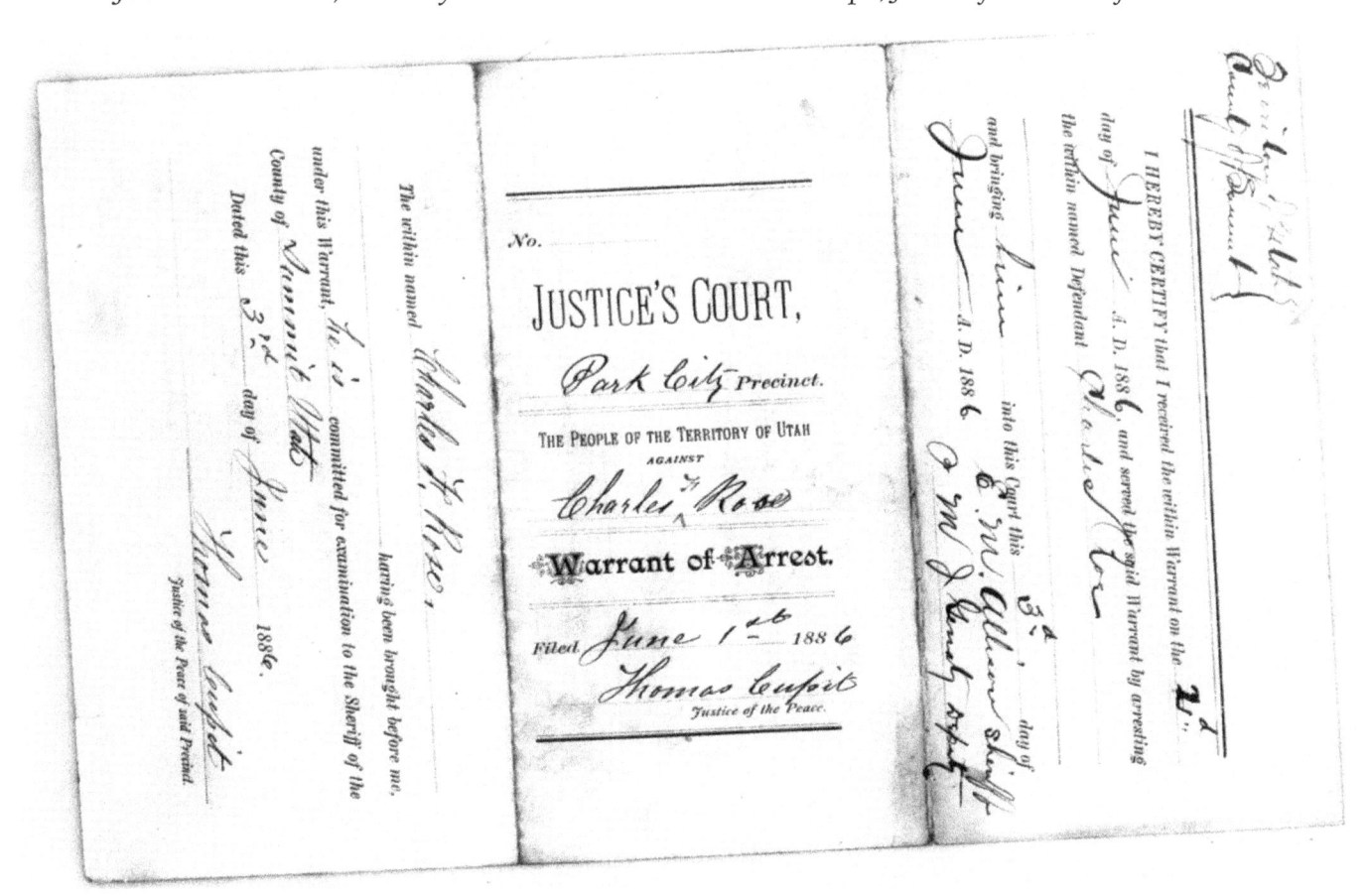

Jubilee Haddessa

JUSTICE'S COURT, Park City Precinct.
The People of the Territory of Utah AGAINST Charles F Rose
Warrant of Arrest.
Filed June 1st, 1886
Thomas Cupit, Justice of the Peace.

Territory of Utah, County of Summit
I HEREBY CERTIFY that I received the within Warrant of the 2nd day of June A.D. 1886, and served the said Warrant by arresting the within named Defendant Charles Rose and bringing him into this Court this 3rd day of June A.D. 1886.
E. M. Allison, Sheriff
PM F. Gerraty, Deputy

Before Thomas Cupit J. P. Park City Precinct, County of Summit, and Territory of Utah.
The People of the Territory of Utah. Plff. vs. Charles F. Rose.Dept.

Be it remembered that on this 1st day of June 1886, Henry Newell, swore to and filed in Court his complaint in charging the defendant Charles F. Rose with committing the crime of Grand Larceny, as follows, by stealing One dark Grey Gelding horse four years old, at Park City, Summit County, Utah Territory on the 29th day of May 1886, of the balance of Fifty Dollars. The personal Property of John F. Allen. On this said 1st day of June 1886. The Court issued Warrant of arrest for said Charles F. Rose and place it in the hands of M. F. Gerraty, Deputy Sheriff of said County under arrest. E. M. Allison Jr Deputy prosecuting Attorney appeared for the People. Complaint read and defendant pleaded not guilty. The following named witnesses was then duly sworn and testified for the People. John F. Allen. Henry Newell and M. F. Gerraty hear the defendant made a motion to be allowed time to get counsel, the Court allowed the defendant with 2 O'Clock PM this said 3rd day of June 1886.

Now at 2 O'Clock P.M. the defendant was again brought into court and H. V. Martin appeared as Counsel for Defendant, and the prosecuting Attorney filed affidavit for a continuance to get the horse stolen and the sheriff of Uinta County, Wyoming Territory, the court granted a continuance until June 7th 1886 at 10 A.M. and admitted the defendant to bail in the sum of $500.00 dollars in default of side bail the defendant was committed to the Custody of the Sheriff of said Summit County, Utah Territory.

Now on this 7th day of June 1886 this examination came on regularly to be hand and by agreement at the Prosecuting Atty with the defendants Atty. John F. Allen. Henry Newell and M. F Gerraty were reexamined on the part of the people also JF. Le Cain sheriff of Uinta County, Wyoming Territory. Who arrested the defendant at Evanston in said County and Territory, on 1st day of June 1886, after these witnesses had testified the prosecution rested except in rebuttal. Witnesses sworn and testified for the defense where the defendant, Wm Archibald. Constantine Gardner, Doctors Lecompte? and F. C. Blanchely?, hear the defense rested and John F. Allen was then called in rebuttal.

The Court after hearing the arguments of Counsels and reviewing the testimony, being of the opinion that the defendant is guilty as Charged in the complaint and that there is sufficient cause to believe the within named Charles F. Rose Guilty. Therefore, order that he be held to answer to the same, and that he is admitted to bail in the sum of Five Hundred dollars and is committed to the sheriff of the County of Summit, Utah Territory, until he gives such bail or is legally discharged.
Thomas Cupit, Justice of the Peace of said Precinct.

Territory of Utah, County of Summit
I the undersigned a Justice of the Peace in and for Park City Precinct Summit County, Utah Territory, do hereby certify that the above and fore going is a complete and true copy or transcript of my docket in the above entitled cause, and the papers hear enclosed is all that I have in my possession.
Dated this 19th day of June 1886.
Thomas Cupit, Justice of the Peace

TERRITORY OF UTAH, County of Summit
IN THE JUSTICE'S COURT. Park City Precinct.
The People of the Territory of Utah:
To John Allen Henry Newell M. J. Gerraty, Wm Archabaild and Doctor LeCompt. Dr. Blackley, J.J. Lecair Constantin Gardner

You are hereby commanded to appear before Thomas Cupit, a Justice of the Peace of Park City Precinct, in the County of Summit at the office of said Justice, in said Precinct, on the 3rd day of June A.D. 1886, at 10 o'clock, A.M. as a witness in a criminal action prosecuted by the people of the Territory of Utah, against Charles F. Rose and for a failure to attend you will be deemed guilty of a contempt of Court.

Given under my hand, this 3rd day of June 1886.
Thomas Cupit, Justice of the Peace of said Precinct.

Criminal Subpoena
For Sale at SALT LAKE HERALD office

Before Thomas Cupit. J. P. Park City Precinct. County of Summit and Territory of Utah.

The People of the Territory of Utah. }
vs. Plffs.
Charles F. Rose. Deft

Be it remembered, that on this 1st day of June 1886. Henry Newell. swore to and filed in court his complaint in writing charging the defendant Charles F. Rose. with committing the crime of Grand Larceny. as follows. by stealing One dark Grey Gelding horse four years old. At Park City. Summit County. Utah Territory. on the 29th day of May 1886. of the value of fifty Dollars. the personal property of One John F. Allen. On this said 1st day of June 1886. the court issued warrant of arrest for said Charles F. Rose. and placed it in the hands of M. J. Gerraty. Deputy Sheriff of said County for service. Now on this 3rd day of June 1886. said Deputy Sheriff. brought said defendant into court under arrest. E. M Allison Jr. Deputy prosecuting Attorney appeared for the People. — Complaint read. and defendant pleaded not guilty. the following named witnesses was then duly sworn and testified for the People. John F. Allen. Henry Newell. and M. J. Gerraty. hear the defendant made a motion. to be allowed time to get counsel the court allowed the defendant until 2 O'clock P.M. this said 3rd day of June 1886. —

Now at 2 O'clock P.M. the defendant was again brought into court. And H. E. Martin appeared as counsel for defendant. And the prosecuting attorney filed affidavit for a continuance, to get the horse stolen, and the sheriff of Uinta County, Wyoming Territory. The court granted a continuance until June 7th 1886. at 10 o. M. and admitted the defendant to bail in the sum of $500 Five hundred dollars, in default of said bail the defendant was committed to the custody of the Sheriff of said Summit County, Utah Territory. —

Now on this 7th day of June 1886. this examination came on regularly to be heard, and by agreement of the prosecuting atty. with the defendants Atty. John F. Allen, Henry Howell, and Mr. J. Gerraty where reexamined on the part of the people also J. J. LeCain. Sheriff of Uinta County, Wyoming Territory. who arrested the defendant at Evanston in said County and Territory, on the 1st day of June 1886. After these witnesses had testified the prosecution rested except in rebutal. Witnesses sworn and testified for the defense, where the defendant. Wm Archibald, Constantine Gardner, Doctors Lecompte and F.C. Blachely, here the defense rested, and John F. Allen was then called in rebutal. —

The Court after hearing the arguments of Counsels

and reviewing the testimony, being of the opinion that the defendant is guilty as charged in the complaint. and that their is sufficient cause to believe the within named Charles F. Rose. Guilty thereof. I Order that he be held to answer to the same. and that he is admitted to bail in the sum of Five Hundred dollars. and is committed to the Sheriff of the County of Summit. Utah Territory. until he gives such bail or is legally discharged.

Thomas Cupit
Justice of the Peace
of Said Precinct

Territory of Utah } ss.
County of Summit

I the undersigned a Justice of the Peace. in and for Park City Precinct. Summit County. Utah Territory, do hereby certify. that the above and foregoing is a complete. and true copy or transcript of my docket in the above entitled cause, and the papers hear enclosed is all that I have in my possession Dated this 19th day of June 1886.

Thomas Cupit
Justice of the Peace

Transcript of Docket

People
vs.
Charles F. Rose

In the Justice Court
Park City Precinct
Summit County Utah.

The People of the Territory
of Utah.
Against
Charles F. Rose

Complaint
Filed June 1st 1886,
Thomas Cussit
Justice of the Peace

In the Justices Court Park City Precinct
County of Summit Territory of Utah

The People of the Territory of Utah }
     vs
Charles F. Rose.   Defendant }

Territory of Utah }
County of Summit } ss

   Henry Newell being first duly sworn on his oath upon information and belief accuses Charles F. Rose of the Crime of Grand Larceny committed as follows, that the said Charles Roe at Park City Precinct in the County of Summit and Territory of Utah on the 29th day of May 1886 one dark grey gelding horse four years old of the value of fifty dollars of the personal property goods and chattels of one John Allen — then and there being found did then and there unlawfully and feloneously take steal lead and drive away, Contrary to the form of the statute in such cases made and provided and against the peace and dignity of the people aforesaid.

       Henry Newell

Subscribed and sworn to before me this 1st day of June. A.D. 1886.

       Thomas Cupit
       Justice of the Peace

TERRITORY OF UTAH.	IN THE JUSTICE'S COURT.
County of Summit ss.	Park City Precinct.

The People of the Territory of Utah:

To John Allen Henry Newell
W. J. Genaty. Wm Archabald. and
Docter Lecompt, Dr Blackley.
J J Lecain Constantin Gardner

You are hereby commanded to appear before Thomas Cupit, a Justice of the Peace of Park City Precinct, in the County of Summit at the office of said Justice, in said Precinct, on the 3rd day of June A. D. 1886, at 10 o'clock, A.M., as a witness in a criminal action prosecuted by the people of the Territory of Utah, against Charles F Rose

and for a failure to attend you will be deemed guilty of a contempt of Court.

Given under my hand, this 3rd day of June 1886.

Thomas Cupit
Justice of the Peace of said Precinct.

Criminal Subpœna.   For Sale at Salt Lake Herald Office.

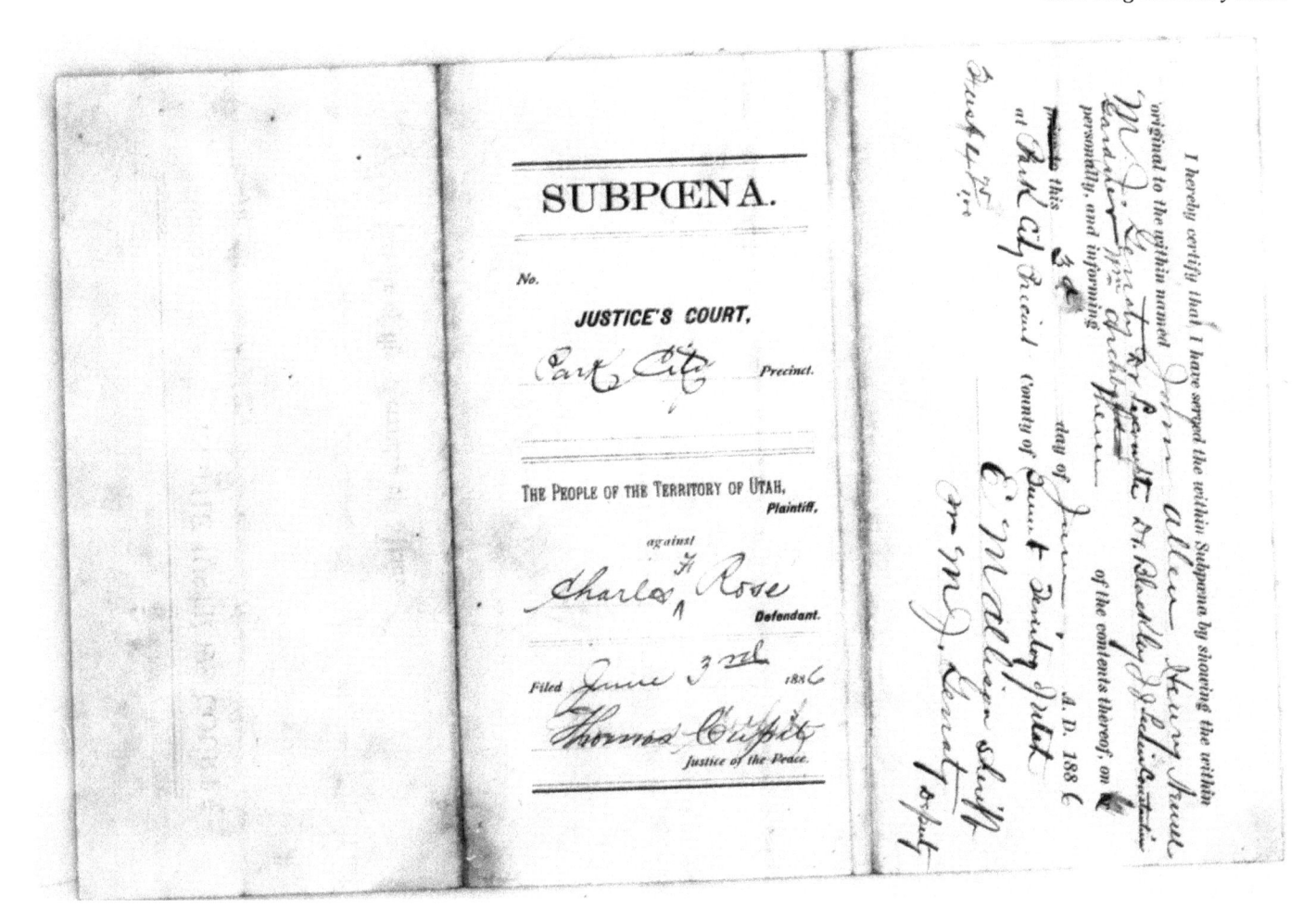

SUBPOENA
JUSTICE'S COURT, Park City Precinct.
The People of the Territory of Utah, Plaintiff, Against Charles F. Rose, Defendant,
Filed June 3rd 1886
Thomas Cupit, Justice of the Peace.

I hereby certify that I have served the within Subpoena by showing the within original to the within named John Allen Henry Newell M. J. Gerraty, and Doctor LeCompt. Dr. Blackley, J.J. Lecair Constantin Gardner Wm Archabaild personally, and informing them of the contents thereof, on this 3rd day of June, A.D. 1886 at Park City Precinct County of Summit Territory of Utah.
Cost 4.75
E. M. Allison, Sheriff, or M.J. Gerraty, Deputy.

Read June 21st 1886
People Vs. Charles Rose
Grand Larceny
John M. Zane 3rd Dist Co
Salt Lake Utah.

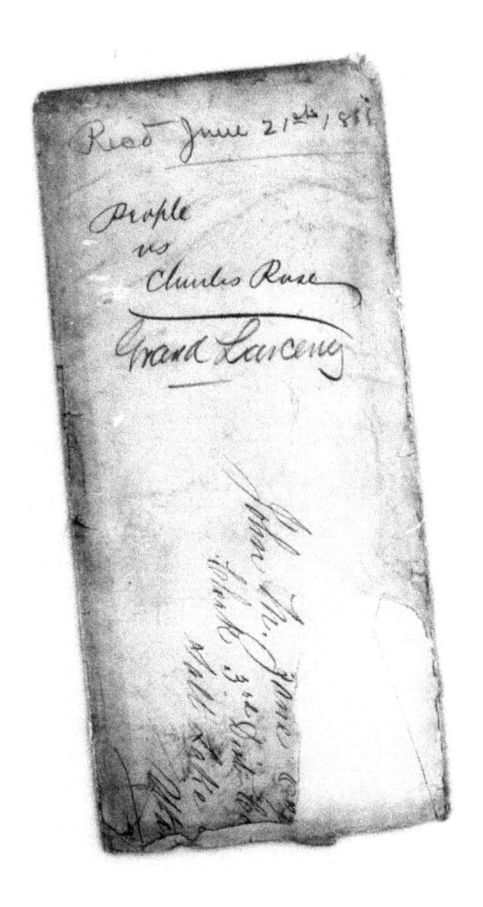

Territory of Utah   } In the Justice's Court of Park
County of Summit   } City Precinct, Before Thomas
Park City Precinct   } Culpit, Justice of the Peace.

The People of the Territory }
of Utah   }
        — vs —   } Affidavit
Charles H. Rose   }

E. M. Allison Jr. being first duly sworn deposes and says:—

I. I am the assistant prosecuting attorney for Summit County.

II. J. J. LeCain, whose residence is Evanston, Uintah County, Wyoming, and _____ whose residence is Evanston, Uintah County, Wyoming are witnesses material and necessary for the people of the Territory in in the prosecution of the above action

III. that this is not made for the purposes of delay or to defeat the ends of justice

E. M. Allison Jr.

Subscribed and sworn to before me this the 3rd day of June A.D. 1886

Thomas Culpit
Justice of the Peace

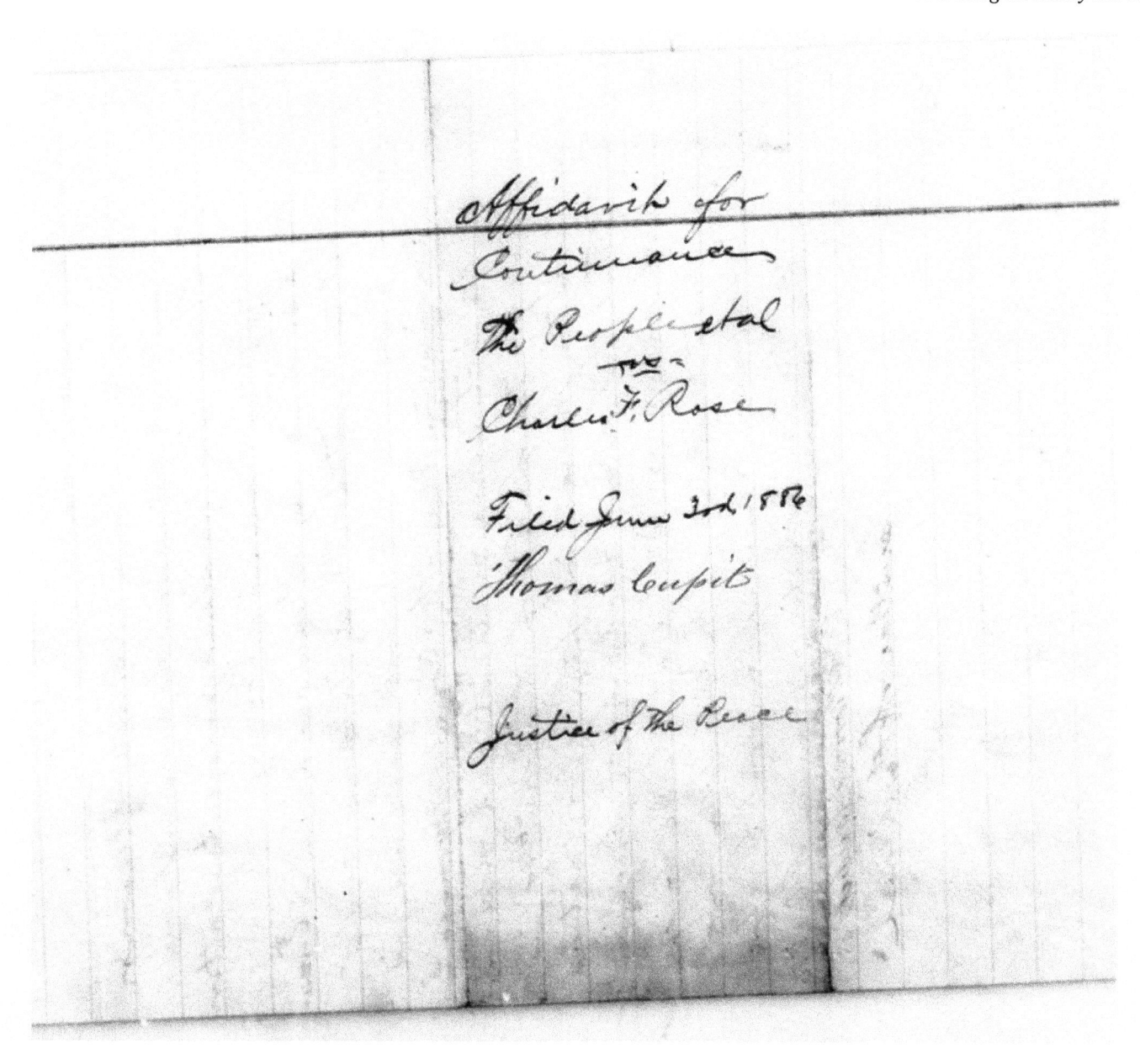

TERRITORY OF UTAH, COUNTY OF SUMMIT
IN THE JUSTICE'S COURT OF PARK CITY PRECINCT
before Thomas Cupit, Justice of the Peace
The People of the Territory of Utah Vs. Charles F. Rose
Affidavit:
E.M. Allison Jr. being first duly sworn deposes and says:
I. I am the assistant prosecuting attorney for Summit County.
II. J.J. Le Cain, whose residence is Evanston, Uintah County, Wyoming, and are witnesses material and necessary for the people of the Territory in in the prosecution of the above action.
III. That this is not made for the purposes of delay or to defeat the ends of justice.
E.M. Allison Jr.
Subscribed and sworn to before me this the 3rd day of June A.D. 1886.
Thomas Cupit, Justice of the Peace.

AFFIDAVIT FOR CONTINUANCE
The People et al Vs. Charles F. Rose
Filed June 3rd 1886
Thomas Cupit, Justice of the Peace

So many questions remain unanswered about Charles F. Rose. He stole a bridle and saddle at one place then stole a Gray Gelding male horse to ride to Evanston, Wyoming, back in the 1800s this was considered Grand Larceny because that is how people got around, mostly on horseback and a man's horse was his livelihood.

I decided to investigate Judge Charles S. Zane and U.S. Marshal Frank Drayer after I found Charles's documents because they were involved in all three of my ancestors' court cases: Sarah Tonge, Peter Tonge, and Charles F. Rose.

This made me very curious. On Familysearch.org, there is a tool you can use to see how you are related to someone up to fifteen generations. Judge Charles S. Zane and Marshal Frank Drayer are both related to me on my mother's side. I find this very funny. It's like one side of my family threw the other side of my family in jail. Poetic justice, really.

I think this would be grounds for a family feud if anyone had known about this story from more than a hundred years ago. I will have to dig more into Judge Zahn and Marshal Drayer's stories. So many stories there, I'm sure.

12 My Experience At 'The Dungeon'

The day after we went to the Utah State Archives, in mid-June 2019, I dropped my sister and her boys off at her friend's house in Salt Lake City at about one in the afternoon. However, I had forgotten which road to take back to Foothill Drive toward Parley's Canyon to go back home. My plans were to investigate the Park City Museum in Park City.

As I was driving, I was talking to my friend Nicole through my hands-free device about my discoveries the day before. I decided just to drive east because that was where Foothill Drive was, and figured I would hit it eventually. I was literally led by my ancestors and ran right into Sugar House Park.

"That is where the Utah Territorial Penitentiary was located," Nicole said. "There is a historical marker there."

I had not even been looking for Sugar House Park. "I don't have time to look for the historical marker today, but I will come back on a different day. I know I was just literally led here while I was driving by an unseen entity. I am on my way to the Park City Museum."

"Peter Tonge was held there overnight, according to the newspaper article 'A Revolting Affair.' "

"I know. That is one of the reasons I am going there." I said. "I will tell you about it later."

The Park City Museum entrance opens into a gift shop. To the back left, there is a large wooden desk, curved like half of a horseshoe. I had to weave past displays to reach the desk to talk to the two ladies on duty. There was not a straight path.

"I heard a rumor that there is a Utah Territorial Prison still downstairs. Is that true?" I asked. "If it is, how can I go see it?"

"It's $12 to go through the museum. Why the interest in 'The Dungeon'?" one of the ladies asked.

"One of my ancestors ended up spending the night down there."

"Was your ancestor a miner?" (As in a miner in the mines of Park City in the late 1880s.)

"No, he was a laborer and English."

I paid to go through the museum, which itself was an interesting and educational experience. When I finally reached The Dungeon's wrought iron barred door, I completely broke down, sobbing my heart and soul out.[68] It was so overwhelmingly emotional just to stand in this doorway. It took me a good five minutes to compose myself before I passed through this doorway to enter the rest of The Dungeon. It was almost as if Peter Tonge was in that place with me.

This is the wrought iron barred door through which you enter The Dungeon.

---

[68] Photos of the "Dungeon" in Park City, Summit County, Utah, United States, (Photos taken by Jubilee Haddessa on 26 June 2019)

It felt like he was so pleased that one of his descendants was actually looking into his life and not judging him for it.

I didn't even have a chance to brace myself for such an emotional response. I felt so overwhelmed by it all. I still do even now, nearly five years later. I still can't explain all the emotions I was feeling that day. They were so strong, like I was feeling all the feelings that Peter Tonge had to have felt on the night he spent there all those years ago.

Betrayal, fear of the unknown, worry for his daughter whom he had tried to hide, worry for his young children at home, and so many more unidentified emotions.

I spent about an hour there, just exploring and trying to process my feelings. I pondered what this prison must have been like in 1888.

The windows next to and below the stairs are smaller than a foot square. They still bear their iron bars.

The jail is very dark, even with electric lights. In the 1800s, there wouldn't have been any electricity; candles would have been used in tandem with natural light.

It would have been *so* dark.

The three smaller cells were about six feet by four feet, and the iron-barred doors were about eight feet tall and only about a foot wide. I could barely fit my shoulders through the door without turning sideways and shuffling in. There were no bunks. I think the prisoners had to sleep on the hard concrete floors. The larger cell was about ten feet by ten feet.

The main room had an old-fashioned toilet inside, open to the air. There was only one small, cast iron potbelly wood burning stove to heat the jail. It looked like the whole jail was only about one hundred to two hundred square feet.

I went back to the gift shop on the main floor up front. I asked the two ladies from before whether they had any records about any of the prisoners that went through The Dungeon.

"No, but there is a book about all the people who died in and around the Park City area," one said.

"I will take it." I bought *Death and Dying in Old Park City* by Gary Kimball and started reading it.

In the introduction, Gary Kimball explains his book's purpose: *"This is a story of the forgotten ones: People who were buried in the cemetery in Park City who, for a variety of reasons, were soon forgotten after burial. . . . No official records exist of their deaths, or the locations of their graves. . . . In 1998, I happened to attend a viewing at Oplin's Funeral Home in Heber. By chance, I asked Guy Oplin if he had records from Archer's Mortuary that was bought by Oplin in the early 1960s. The answer was yes, and he was generous enough to share them with me. From these records I found over 200 deaths not recorded in the Park City Cemetery. Thinking I might double the number by checking the files of the Park Record newspaper, I stumbled into a project that would take over 18 months to complete.*

. . . After a month or so, it dawned on me that many of the death notices and obituaries were 'time capsules,' mini-biographic stories, much more powerful and moving than a mere death list."

I feel like I had met a kindred spirit in Gary Kimball as I read those words. I, too, have stumbled upon a project I am very passionate about. It's a project that will probably be a lifelong quest.

Remember that prisoner roster I had from the Utah State Archives? Well, I had also come to realize that all the information that was written down there was also like a "snapshot" of a prisoner's life. These are people who were likely forgotten and considered expendable. I will also be writing a collaboration about these people, for they mattered at least to one person—me.

One day in the fall of 2019, I was going back through the books and documents I had gotten from the Park City Museum. On the back of the museum's brochure, it stated that there was a research center in the basement. On one side of the basement was The Dungeon and on the other was the research center. I have no idea how I had missed the research center the first time, but I needed to go explore it. I just had to figure out a time to go back there. This was huge. I had so many questions to ask about cemetery records, where the railroads used to be in the Park City area, and other topics.

A bolt of lightning—an epiphany, really—struck my brain at that moment. All my research was leading me back to that same list of Utah and Wyoming cities, especially the Utah Territorial Prison System. I was becoming somewhat of an expert in this area.

There was—okay, is—a compulsion to learn everything I could about the system and the people that were involved or incarcerated in it. My epiphany was that I needed to become an accredited professional genealogist, specializing in the Utah Territorial Prison System. I submitted a Four Generational Research Paper to ICAPGen for the first level accreditation in fall of 2020 with these same people as the research topic. I failed, however, because I needed more education in how they wanted the report written.

I enrolled myself in BYU-Idaho's Professional Studies Bachelor's of Science Degree in the winter of 2021. This is a fully online degree. (I tried enrolling in BYU-Provo, Utah's. Family History Research Bachelors of Science Degree but as I already had a BS Degree from a different University I couldn't enroll there. So, BYU-Idaho it was for an online degree) Three Certificates are needed for a Professional Studies Degree; I chose Family History Research Certificate, Advanced Family History Research Certificate, and a Certificate in Entrepreneurship. I have completed the first Family History Research certificate. I am two classes away from my Advanced Family History Certificate and have five or classes for Entrepreneurship. I am only taking one class a semester three semesters a year because of life's demands.

I have maybe two and a half years left, since all my generals transferred over from my other Bachelor of Science degree. Two years ago, I also started my own family history research business. As of now, I have four active clients. Writing family history books has also helped me along this path to becoming an accredited professional genealogist. Once I am done with school, I will focus on the accreditation process through ICAPGen again, starting with a rewrite of the Four Generational Paper now that I know how they want it written.

This story has inspired me to help others find their ancestors and the forgotten people. All people matter. All people deserve their stories to be told. I know from personal experience what it is like to be forgotten or overlooked. No one should feel that way. No one is expendable. We are all human, and we all bleed red.

13 Investigating In Wasatch County

The 1900 census told us about Maude's younger half-brother, Jay Spratley Sabey. Well, my friend and I found a few newspaper articles from 1896 that shed more light on the time leading up to the census. One article, called "Fun In the Heber Court," discussed the court case of Jedidiah Spratley vs. Sarah Targe on a charge of fornication.[69] Sarah's last name was spelled Targe in this article. However, we know that this was actually Sarah Tonge because the article mentions Wallsburg, Heber City and American Fork, which tracked with Sarah Tonge's coming and goings during 1896.

We had found the father of Jay Spratley Sabey. It would seem that Sarah's affair with Mr. Jedidiah Spratley was a rebound relationship. I believe she loved Charles F. Rose, and his disappearance after Roy was either conceived or after Roy's birth in 1892 hurt her deeply. After all, there is a very fine line between love and hate.

While at the Utah State Archives in mid-June 2019, the same day that I found Charles F. Rose's court case, I had asked the staff if they had any court cases for Jed Spratley and Sarah Tonge. They said they did not have any in the State Archives, but they might be records at the county level. They recommended the Wasatch County Recorder's Office, so that was my next stop while researching the Spratley side. I would have to go to the Wasatch County Recorder's Office another day. As my sister and two of her boys were with me and we had plans.

So the next day after I had dropped them off at my sister's friend's place and after I left the Park City Museum, for the Wasatch County Recorder's Office in Heber City on a mission to find information on the Tonges or anything on James Sabey or Jed Spratley in relation to Sarah before they closed at 5pm.

---

69 University of Utah. "Fun In the Heber Court," images, Newspapers.lib.utah Database, (https://www.newspapers.lib.utah.edu: accessed 5 August 2024,) Salt Lake Tribune (Salt Lake City, Salt Lake County, Utah, USA), 24 July 1896, page 3.

HEBER COURT.

An Error That Made a Highly Important Difference.

Heber City, July 23—Correspondence Tribune—In the case of the State vs. Jed Spratley, called today, fornication is charged, at Wallsburg with Sarah Targe, on or about July 27, 1895. The defense announced readiness for trial, having found that the prosecution had filed two informations, one laying the offense on June 27, 1896, and one on July, 27, 1896, an error of a year. On the prosecution being asked to choose which information they would rely upon, they said the one of July 27, 1896. Defense promptly asked dismissal because that date had not yet arrived, and was an impossible one for a crime.

The prosecution claimed the right to amend, admitting error of a year, and the defense contested, the court holding, after a long argument by counsel, that inasmuch as under the old Territorial law in cases of this kind the grand jury was permitted to bring in an amended indictment, he would allow the prosecution to bring in a new information.

While the new paper was preparing, the defense announced that they would not be prepared to go to trial on the new time; they couldn't account all at once for a year's conduct.

The court ordered that the defendant be arraigned; he was at work at Mercur, and there was no response to the calling of his name. His counsel claimed the right to answer for him, but as imprisonment might follow conviction on the charge, the court denied such right, and the bond was declared forfeited.

Jury discharged for term.

In the Midway irrigation case, statement of account demanded, which involves ten days' delay, and continuance.

Kinsey vs. Bakery, obstructing highway, no jury demanded; will be tried by court, and may be compromised.

John A Thomas vs. Archer Sellars; damage to a horse, which Sellars's sons are claimed to have inflicted last December by driving into the animal as he was racing. Plaintiff given judgment for $10.

The Wasatch County Recorder's office is in the Wasatch County Offices building.[70]

This brown brick building with a white roof is three stories, one of which is the basement where the assessor and DMV registration offices are. The recorder's office is on the top floor. The building sits on Main Street and Center Street in Heber City which is the county seat. I walked up the large cement staircase lined with wrought iron banisters out front, then turned left. Once I entered the recorder's office, I spotted a tall, light-colored wooden reception desk. Both the people working at the office and those who came to get help must stand up to see over it.

I told the staff that I was there to do some family history research, so they led me through the locked gate to the left of the desk. The next room, called "The Vault," is where they keep all of Wasatch County's land records. There is a large wooden table, about waist height, in the middle of the room, computers and a large printer on one wall, and bookshelves filled with large, red hardback ledger books on another. Each one of those books was about fourteen inches tall and four inches thick. The earliest one was dated 1862, the year Wasatch County was formed.

Several index books made it simpler to look for a particular person. All of the land records were also on microfiche, with a microfiche reader and computer screen that allows you to print off the land records nearby.[71] Printed copies are a dollar each, but worth it because it is hard to read a microfiche on the screen. The document's colors are reversed when viewed on the screen.[72]

The office had some records on James Sabey and Sarah Tonge, but they did not have any records on adoptions or the court cases. I found a Warranty Deed of James and Sarah Sabey from the year 1908, where they sold about forty acres to C.H. Taylor and C.W. Glazier and their Homestead patent for the Sabey Homestead near Wallsburg, Utah, for the year 1893. These two documents helped me firmly place James and Sarah Sabey in and around Wallsburg after their marriage.

---

70 Photo of the Wasatch County Administration Offices on 25 N. Main Street Heber City, Utah. (https://www.kpcw.org/wasatch-county/2022-08-22/wasatch-county-seeks-more-time-to-appraise-homes-balance-assessmen Accessed 11 July 2024).

71 Photo of Microfiche, (https://i.etsystatic.com/7140759/r/il/a39849/2464243987/il_fullxfull.2464243987_53de.jpg Accessed 22 July 2024).

72 Photo of Microfiche Reader, (https://www.repairmanual.com/product/microfiche/ Accessed 22 July 2024).

Entry No. 14927
WARRANTY DEED[73]

James Saby and Sarah Saby his wife, grantors of Wallsburg, County of Wasatch, State of Utah, hereby COVEY –AND WARRANT – to C. H. Taylor and C. W. Glazier grantees of the same place for the sum of Twenty DOLLARS, the following described tract of land in Wasatch County, State of Utah all of that portion of the West half of the Southeast granter of Section three (3) in Township five (5) South of Range four (4) East of the Salt Lake meridian, lying south of the North Bank of Wallsburg Creek, together with a strip of land four (4) rods wide along the East side

---

[73] Wasatch County, Utah, USA, "Warranty Deed James Sabey and Sarah Tonge," Wasatch County Recorder's Office, Heber City, Wasatch, Utah, USA. (Accessed: 23 Jun 2019) Photocopies in the position of the preparer. From Books B. Certificate number: 149.
Wasatch County, Utah, USA, "The Homestead Patent of James Sabey and Sarah Tonge," Wasatch County Recorder's Office, Heber City, Wasatch, Utah, USA. (Accessed: 23 Jun 2019) Photocopies in the position of the preparer. From Book P. Certificate number: 44908.

of said West half of the section three, extending from the North bank of said creek North to the County Road between Charlston and Wallsburg.

Area about forty Acres, more or less.

WITNESS the hands of said grantors this the fourth day of April A.D. nineteeen Hundred and (6) Six.

James Saby
Sarah Saby
Signed in the presence of Daniel Bigelow

STATE OF UTAH, County of Wasatch

On the fourth day of April A.D. nineteen hundred and six personally appeared before me, James Sabey and Sarah Sabey his wife the signer of the above instrument, who duly acknowledge to me that they exucuted the same.

My commission expires Apr 18, 1908

Daniel Bigelow, Notary Publc

Reconded at request of C.H. Taylor, April 5 1906, at 1 o'clock P.M,. in Book "6" of Deeds and Transfers, page 56, Records of Wastach County, Utah. Abstracted 5/4 Page 3. Line 2.

Recording fee .70 Cents

Chas. J. Wahlquest, County Recorder

In this document, Sabey is spelled Saby, but they are the correct James and Sarah Sabey because this is land in and around Wallsburg, where James and Sarah lived.[74]

Transcript:

#14908
The United States of America
Homestead Certificate No. 4821
Application 7104.

To all to whom these presents shall come, greeting: Whereas there has been deposited with General Land Office of the United States a Certificate of the Register of the Land Office at Salt Lake City, Utah Territory, whereby it appears that, pursuant to the Act of Congress approved 20th May 1862, "To secure Homestead to Actual Settlers on the Public Domain", and the acts supplemental there to, the Claim of James Saby has been established and duly consummated, in conformity to law/for the South half of the South East Quarter, the North West Quarter of the South East Quarter of section three, in Township for South of Range Four East of the Salt Lake Meridian, in Utah Territory, obtaining one hundred and sixty acres according to the Official Plat of the survey of the said land, returned to the General Land Office by the Surveyor General.

Now know ye, That there is, therefore, granted by the United States unto the said James Saby the tract of Land above described, to have and to hold the said tract of land, with the appurtenances forever subject to any vested, and accrued water rights for mining, agricultural, magnification, or other purposes, and hights to ditches and reservoirs used in connection with such water and rights, as may be recognized and acknowledged by the local customs, laws, and decisions of courts, and also subject to the right of proprietor of a vein or lode to extract and remove his ore therefrom, should the same be found to penetrate or intersect the premises hereby granted, as provided by law. In testimony whereof, I, Benjamin Harrison, President of the United States of America, have caused the letters to be made patent, and the seal of the General Land Office to be hereunto of fix.

Given under my hand, at the City of Wallsburg, the first day of February, on the year of our Lord one thousand eight hundred and ninety three, and of the Independence of the United States the one hundred and seventeenth.

By the President,
Benjamin Harrison
By E. MacFarland Asst, Secretary
D.P. Roberts.
Records of the General Land Office

Recorded, Vol. 11, Page 184
Recorded at the request of James Saby March 28th 1906 at 12 noon in Book "P" of Patents, Page 507
Chas. J. Wahlquest, County Recorder

This homestead was near the Wallsburg Bay of the Deer Creek Reservoir, according to the Warranty Deed that stated the land sold was near Wallsburg Creek, which empties out into the Wallsburg Bay.[75] It was there long before the reservoir was put in.

---

74 Wasatch County, Utah, USA, "Warranty Deed James Sabey and Sarah Tonge," Wasatch County Recorder's Office, Heber City, Wasatch, Utah, USA. (Accessed: 23 Jun 2019) Photocopies in the position of the preparer. From Books B. Certificate number: 149.

75 Wasatch County, Utah, USA, "The Homestead Patent of James Sabey and Sarah Tonge," Wasatch County Recorder's Office, Heber City, Wasatch, Utah, USA. (Accessed: 23 Jun 2019) Photocopies in the position of the preparer. From Book P. Certificate number: 44908.

Patent

The United States of America

Homestead Certificate No. 2891
Application No. 184

To all to whom these presents shall come, Greeting:

Whereas There has been deposited in the General Land Office of the United States a Certificate of the Register of the Land Office at Salt Lake, Utah Territory, whereby it appears that, pursuant to the Act of Congress approved 20th May, 1862, "To secure Homesteads to Actual Settlers on the Public Domain," and the acts supplemental thereto, the claim of James Saby has been established and duly consummated, in conformity to law, for the South half of the South West quarter, the north west quarter of the South East quarter, and the South East quarter of the South West quarter of Section three, in Township four South of Range four East of Salt Lake Meridian, in Utah Territory, containing one hundred and sixty acres, according to the Official Plat of the Survey of the said land, returned to the General Land Office by the Surveyor General.

Now know ye, That there is, therefore, granted by the United States unto the said James Saby the tract of land above described; To have and to hold the said tract of land, with the appurtenances thereof, unto the said James Saby and to his heirs and assigns forever; subject to any vested and accrued water rights for mining, agricultural, manufacturing, or other purposes, and rights to ditches and reservoirs used in connection with such water rights, as may be recognized and acknowledged by the local customs, laws, and decisions of courts, and also subject to the right of the proprietor of a vein or lode to extract and remove his ore therefrom, should the same be found to penetrate or intersect the premises hereby granted, as provided by law.

In testimony whereof, I, Benjamin Harrison, President of the United States of America, have caused these letters to be made Patent, and the seal of the General Land Office to be hereunto affixed.

Given under my hand, at the City of Washington, the first day of February, in the year of our Lord one thousand eight hundred and ninety three, and of the Independence of the United States the one hundred and seventeenth.

By the President:
Benjamin Harrison
By M. McFarland, Asst. Secretary
D. P. Roberts
Recorder of the General Land Office

Recorded Vol. 11 Page 184.

Recorded at request of James Saby March 28th, 1906 at 12 Noon in Book "P" of Patents page 507.
Chas. S. Wahlquist
County Recorder

The large red arrow is where I think the Sabey Homestead was. The little red arrow is the road (West Main Canyon Road) that leads to Wallsburg Township.

Now, the Sabey Homestead is most likely underwater, just like the old railroad that ran down the middle of the Deer Creek Reservoir. That railroad was moved to the side of the reservoir when they made it in the 1930s.[76]

The homestead has most likely been underwater since Deer Creek Reservoir was filled in 1941.[77] I might be wrong on where the Sabey Homestead was; I will need to find some old maps of Wasatch County just to be sure.

The lady who helped me at the Wasatch County Recorder's Office told me that the Wasatch County Courthouse might have adoption records for Maude, Roy and Jay.

The courthouse might also have the Jed. Spratley vs. Sarah Targe or Tonge court case as well.

A trip to the Wasatch County Courthouse to ask about the adoption records was in order. The courthouse is located on South U.S. 40 near the hospital and the county jail. Three archways under the Wasatch County Courthouse sign lead you toward the tan building's front doors.

---

76 Utah State Parks, "Map of Deer Creek State Park", (https://stateparks.utah.gov/stateparks/wp-content/uploads/sites/26/2015/02/deercreek_dcspoverview.png: Accessed 9 March 2024) Image on the internet. Wikipedia, "Deer Creek State Park, Utah", database with image, Wikipedia, (https://en.wikipedia.org/wiki/Deer_Creek_State_Park_(Utah) Accessed: 10 August 2024). History of Deer Creek State Park.

77 Wikipedia, "Deer Creek State Park, Utah", database with image, Wikipedia, (https://en.wikipedia.org/wiki/Deer_Creek_State_Park_(Utah) Accessed: 10 August 2024). History of Deer Creek State Park

Everyone who enters the courthouse must go through the metal detectors manned by a sheriff's deputy. Once finished with that single-file process, I headed to the right toward the court archives. I talked to a woman there through glass at what looked like a ticket window. Only authorized people are allowed back into the archives; it is off-limits to the general population.

I asked her about the court case of Jed Spratley vs. Sarah Targe or Tonge (I wanted to make sure she looked under both last names). I also wanted to see if there were any adoption papers for Maude, Roy, and Jay to make James Sabey their father legally. The woman asked me to give her a few days to look and said she would call me with the results.

About three days later, she left me a voicemail. There was no court record for Sarah Tonge vs. Jed Spratley at the Wasatch County Courthouse. There were also no adoption records for Maude, Roy or Jay. The woman went on to say that adoptions usually weren't a legal

Wasatch County Courthouse

process in the late 1800s. The man would just say that those were his children and would raise them as his own. No one would bat an eye at that.

There might not be any adoption records at all. There was one last place to look for the court case or the adoption records—the Utah County Courts in Provo, Orem, or American Fork.

14 Why Did Charles Come To the U.S.?

Time for another visit to the Family History Library in Salt Lake City. I wanted to see whether I could figure out when Charles F. Rose came over to the United States from Germany, which was actually Prussia at the time. Before Germany was Prussia, it was a bunch of warring states.

All I was armed with was that Charles F. Rose had been in the Utah Territory between 1886 and about 1892. There were signs that he disappeared from Sarah Tonge's life when she was either pregnant with Roy or shortly after she gave birth to Roy. Or, he could have disappeared between 1892 and 1896, since Jay was born in 1896. Charles was not Jay's biological father.

I have a few theories, but they are just that—theories:

Charles's past may have caught up to him. I think he went back on the run with his old outlaw crew. I think this gang was based out of Evanston, Wyoming. That is where Charles had a shootout with the U.S. Marshals in 1886.

I think Charles told Sarah, newly released from prison and pregnant in April 1888, to go to Evanston and he would meet her there when he was released a few months later in January 1889. Sarah also had relatives from her mother's side (Barnes) there.

Sarah and Charles had at least two children together that I can prove: Maude and Roy. I also believe in my heart that the deformed baby that Sarah had given birth to before being arrested in January 1888 was theirs as well.

How was this possible when Charles was imprisoned in August 1886? Charles could have either escaped for a time or somehow had gotten into the work release program. According to the prisoner roster microfilm I have, prisoners escaped a lot. Sometimes, they were recaptured the same day, sometimes not until days later.[78] There are also rumors that a work release program was implemented for nonviolent prisoners, where prisoners could go work somewhere and had a curfew to be back to the penitentiary before the U.S. Marshals would be sent to rearrest them. Both Sarah and Charles were residents of Snyderville, Utah. That is the outskirts of Park City, and they probably ran in the same circles.

Sarah and Charles never married; if perhaps they did, I have not been able to find any marriage record for them.

Charles could have just decided one day that family life wasn't for him and left them.

Charles could have decided that he did want to go straight, but his former crew found him. They could have taken him out into the desert to kill him for turning on them or for leaving their gang. After all, this was the Wild West.

More research is constantly being conducted on all of the above theories. So far, there has been no death record or grave found for Charles F. Rose. It's like all traces of him just evaporated about 1892.

My goal by coming back to the Family History Library in Salt Lake City was to figure out how Charles had ended up in Utah before his arrest in 1886 and to see whether I could figure out what happened to him after 1892.

The sister missionary that helped me that day found a C.F. Ross on the passenger list of a ship that came from Europe to New York in 1876.[79]

---

78 Utah State Archive. "Prison Commitment Registers," Images, Utah State Archives, Salt Lake City, Salt Lake, Utah, USA, (http://www.archives.utah.org : accessed 12 June 2019), Microfilm: Reel 2 of series 80388, Prison Commitment Registers.

79 Ancestry, "New York Passenger and Crew Lists (including Castle Garden and Ellis Island), 1820-1957", database with images, Ancestry.com, (www.ancestry.com Accessed: 22 June 2019). Entry for C. F. Ross, b.1856, Arrival to the U.S.A. year 1876, Microfilm #: M237, 675 Rolls, NAI: 6256867. Records of the U. S. Customs Service, National Archives at Washington D.C.

Unraveling the Family Secret

He was traveling alone. His last name was Ross instead of Rose, which could be because a lot of people changed their last names when they immigrated to the United States at the time. The port he had come from was in the Netherlands in Holland, which borders Germany.

He was twenty years old, which tracks with Charles being thirty in 1886 when he was arrested. The warm feeling that I felt the day I found Charles F. Rose on the Utah Territorial Penitentiary prisoner roster filled me from head to toe a second time. I knew that this C.F. Ross was the same person as Charles F. Rose.

"It's like he was running from the law even before he came to the United States," I said to the sister missionary.

She wasn't very helpful after I said that. "Now you are just twisting the story to fit the documents."

"No, I am not," I continued. "I know I have a lot more research to do to find his family, but this is him on this passenger list. I just need to figure out how he got to Utah from New York. Plus you just don't wake up one day and steal a horse. You work up to stuff like that."

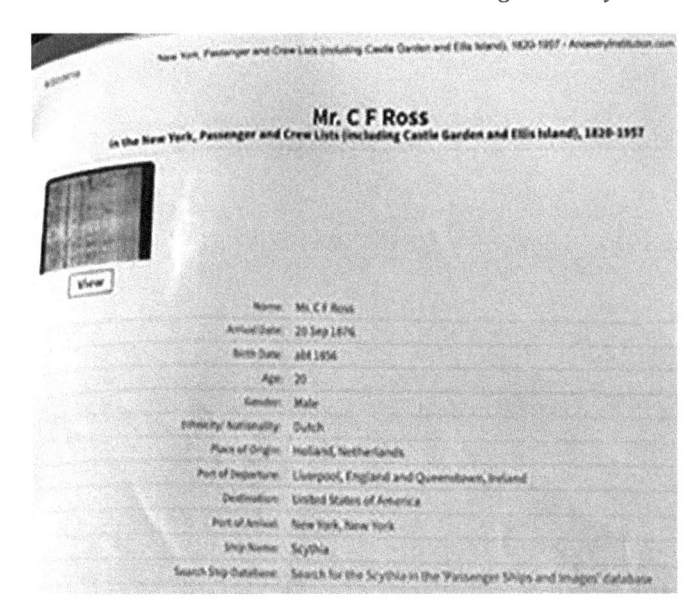

She got up and left in a hoff after that. This sister missionary was not as helpful as other missionaries at the Family History Library in Salt Lake have been in the past.

I didn't let her attitude get me down or discourage me; it just made me do more research. It lit a new fire in my soul.

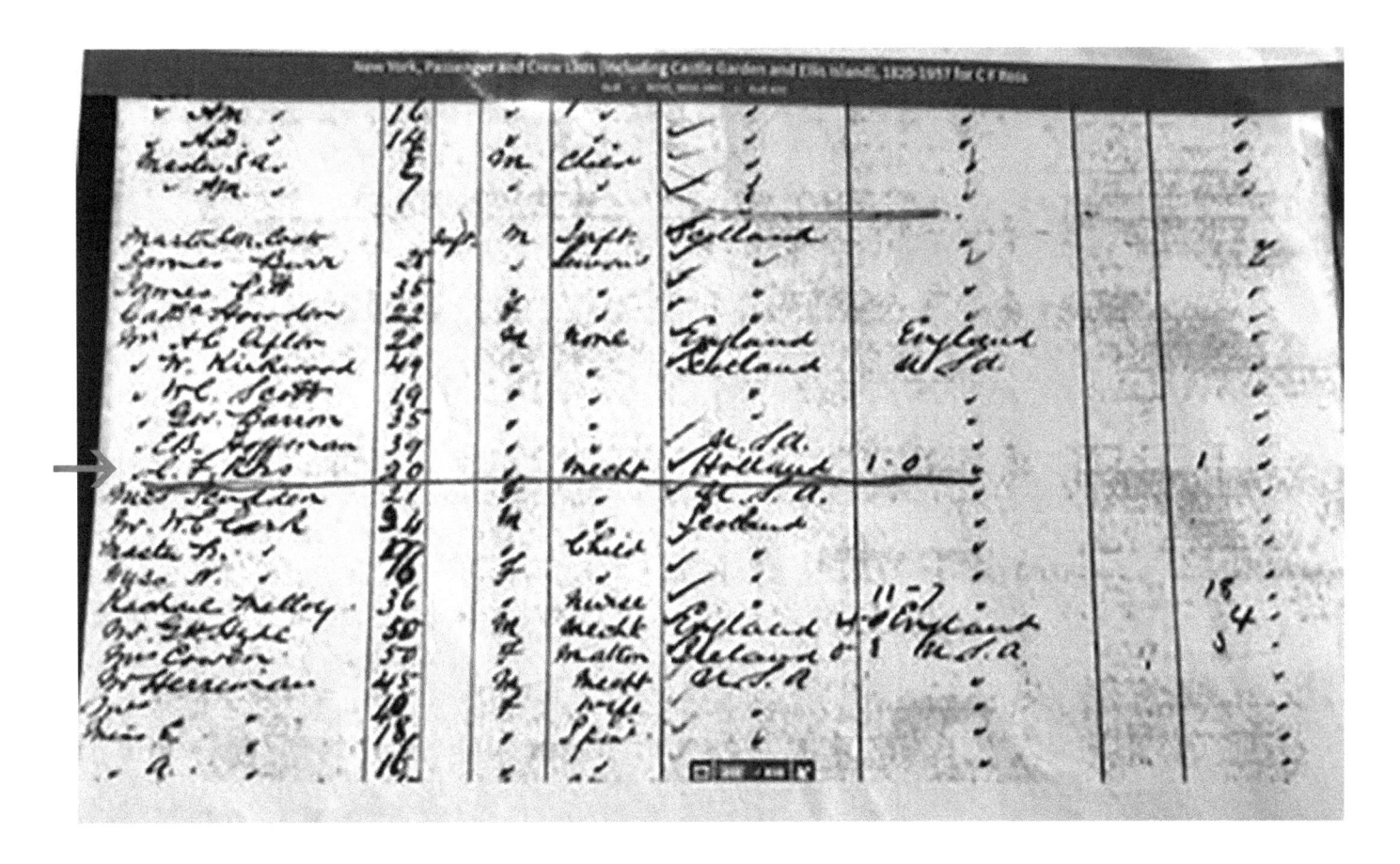

Jubilee Haddessa

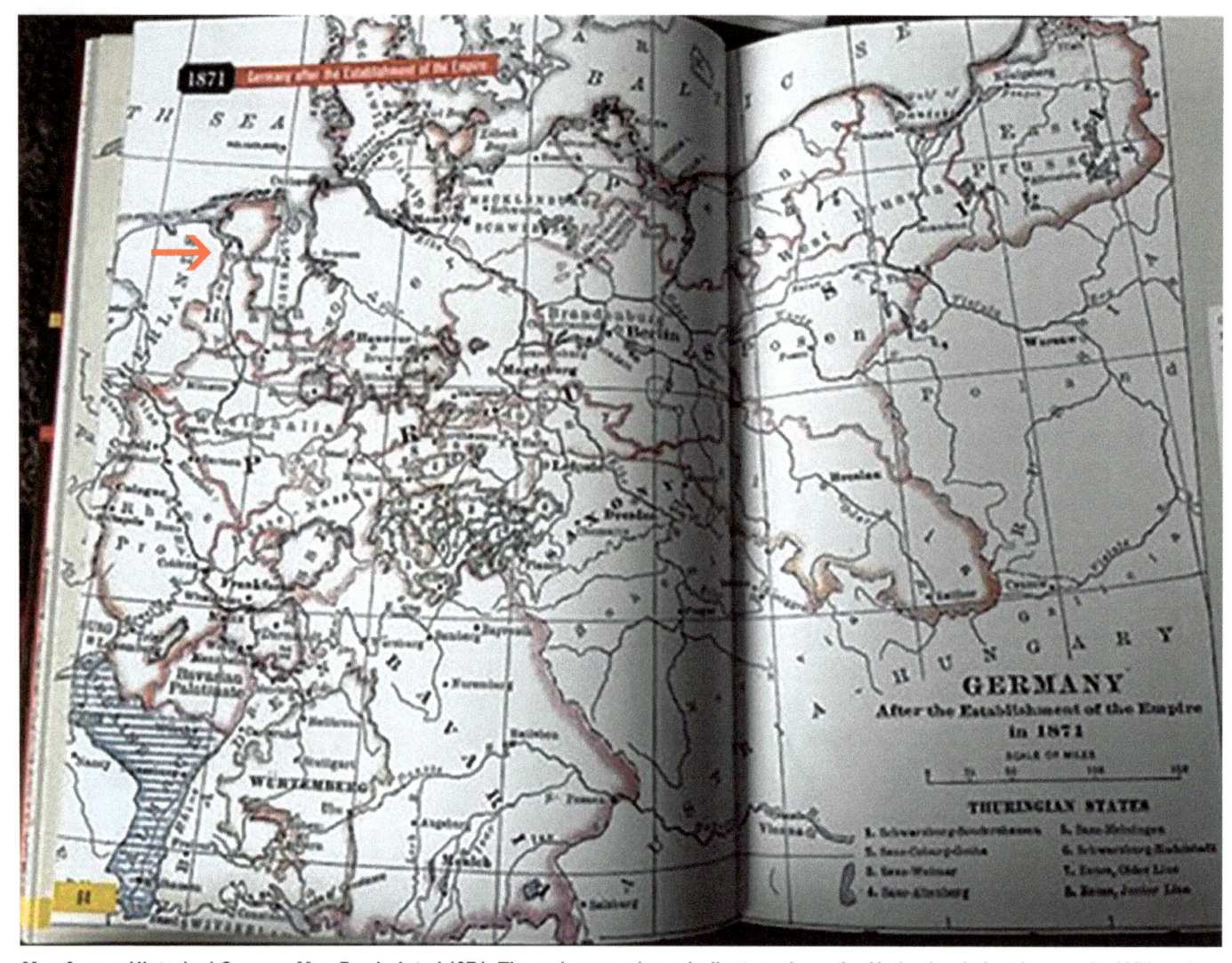

Map from a Historical German Map Book dated 1871. The red arrow above indicates where the Netherlands border was in 1871 and the border of Prussia, Germany. That border has fluctuated a lot over the last thousand years.

I am still researching Charles F. Rose's time in the United States, and I am looking for the rest of his family. Apparently, to do German family history research, you need to know the German hometown of the person being researched. Rose could also be spelled several ways in German: Ruskin, Ruse, Ross, Roz, Rosen, Rosa, etc.[80] That is so frustrating. So, the search will be long and hard, with dead end after dead end. That portion has been a lot like my ten-year search for Charles to begin with.

When I attended RootsTech 2020, a giant family history conference held in Salt Lake City, I met an elderly woman who had fled Germany as a child during World War II. We got to talking about each of our German ancestors, and I showed her the passenger document. She told me that the German word "knecht" under C.F.'s occupation meant "servant." That just deepened the mystery surrounding him. Did Charles steal something valuable from his previous employers in Germany and then flee to the United States to avoid the law? Then, just ten years later, the long arm of the law put him in the Utah Territorial Penitentiary. That is so ironic, really. Outlaws either end up in jail or dead . . . eventually.

---
80 James M. Beidler, *The Family Tree Historical Atlas of Germany*, (Cincinnati, Ohio: Family Tree Books-Patty Craft, 2019, Pages 84-85.

15 Sugar House Park Visit

I do not remember the exact date when I decided to hunt down the historical marker for the Utah Territorial Penitentiary at the Sugar House Park, I do remember it was in the fall of 2019. The park encompasses several city blocks. I drove around it a few times before I finally spotted the two freestanding stone walls through the pine trees. I was so emotional as I parked the car and walked up to the walls, tears running freely down my face. A flood of emotions overwhelmed me. Three of my ancestors had been incarcerated on this site. It was a very sobering experience. Those two stone walls, each only about eight feet tall, and the plaques embedded in these walls were all that was left of the original structure of the Utah Territorial Penitentiary.[81] There was a somber feeling at that location; it was almost as if I was standing on sacred ground. It is very hard to describe what I felt standing at that site.

The women usually were housed in the warden's home with his family. However, by the late 1800s, the prison was overcrowded with both men and women, allowing them to co-mingle.

There is also a potter's field there in the park somewhere dating from the time of the penitentiary. At least a few of the people who were buried there were dug up and reburied in the Salt Lake City Pioneer Cemetery when the prison was relocated to Point of the Mountain (near Draper and Lehi, Utah). They might not have found all the people who were buried there. I have not been able to find the exact location of this potter's field or any burial records for it. It might even be where Sarah Tonge's deformed baby was buried.

However, there are several places that the Tonge family could have buried this child: the Park City area, Heber City or the Salt Lake City area. Research is still being done on this.

---

81 Sugar House Park in Salt Lake City, Salt Lake County, Utah, United States, photos of the Historical Marker of the Utah Territorial Penitentiary taken by Jubilee Haddessa on 29 June 2019.

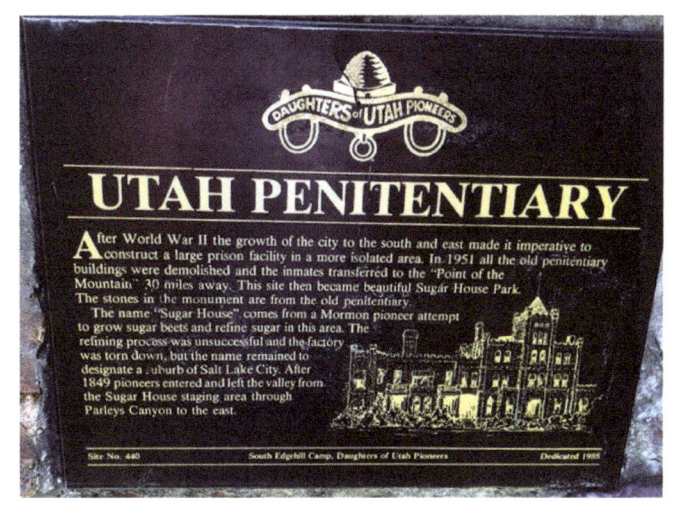

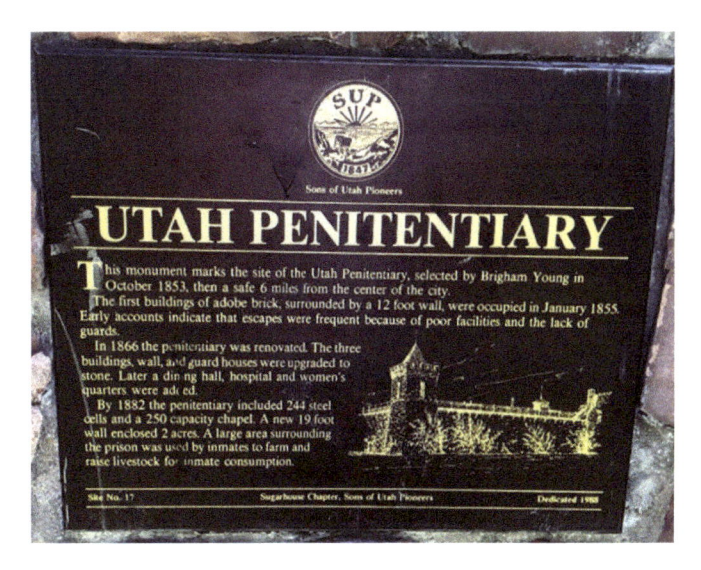

My friend Nicole sent me a long article about the Utah Territorial Penitentiary. Its bibliography pages mentioned that other members of the Church of Jesus Christ of Latter-day Saints who had been imprisoned there for polygamy had written journals during their sentences.[82] This discovery sparked many questions in my head. If Rudger Clawson had written down names of other prisoners during his time in jail, then other prisoners could have done the same thing. Maybe one of them had written down Charles's name and the name of his hometown in Germany.

Another trip to the Family History Library in Salt Lake City was in order. I brought the article about the penitentiary and asked the gentlemen at the front desk whether any of the articles mentioned in its bibliography were there in the library.

He told me the articles would most likely be in the Church History Library, which is next to the Conference Center on the east side of Temple Square. I had never heard of that library before, despite it being just a couple of blocks from the Family History Library. It is dedicated to the preservation of the history of the members of the Church of Jesus Christ of Latter-day Saints.

It is home to a treasure trove of information about the Utah Territorial Penitentiary through those journals. Polygamy charges were what earned the penitentiary its nickname—the Mormon Polygamy Prison. People forget that there were also actual criminals in the penitentiary. About eighty percent of the prisoners held in the prison were actual criminals, while the other twenty percent were polygamists.

Many Saturdays after that were spent at the Church History Library doing research. This library is not as large as the Family History Library. It is only about two stories, plus maybe a basement. I couldn't be sure, as patrons are only allowed on the main floor. The rest of the library is dedicated to restricted archives. As you walk in the main doors, the main foyer has about six large computer desks as well as people ready to help you. The next room includes more books and more computer desks, where patrons can search the library's computer database of its collections. On the right is a taller desk where you can request one microfilm or box of documents from the person behind the desk. Beyond that is a reading room where everyone is supposed to be quiet; no food or drinks are allowed. There were several mahogany-colored tables and a handful of computers with microfilm readers attached, plus a main desk where the library staff would bring the items you requested, one at a time.

I gained a lot of knowledge about how the Utah Territorial Penitentiary was run and the everyday lives of the prisoners incarcerated there, thanks to the physical copies and microfilm copies of the prisoners' journals.

I even found a series of four microfilms that was a duplicate of another set I had found earlier. I wish I had had a camera to capture the reaction of the front desk clerk when I told her about the duplicates. They were under different names and call numbers, but they were definitely the same films. She thanked me profusely and said that I was just cleaning up their shelves and fixing their inventory.

The duplicated films contained a lot of general information about the Utah Territory. One was all about the pardons handed out by the governors of the Utah Territory in the mid- to late 1800s. I saved a copy to my Google Drive. It was fascinating; it gave me more insight into the prisoners and why they were in prison in the first place.

There was one pardon that had captured my attention. It had two names on it: William Rose and Charley Rose. They had been incarcerated for house breaking in 1883 and were pardoned in 1884 and 1886. For a good five minutes, I stared at the computer screen and debated whether this Charley Rose was my Charles F. Rose. What were the odds? I printed the record off and later went back to the Utah State Archives to find the court cases that matched up with the pardon.

However, William and Charley's last name was Ross, not Rose, on the court documents. At the time, I thought that gave me more proof that Charles had changed his name to Rose from Ross after he had arrived in the United States in 1876. But, before I could verify anything, I lost the flash drive that I had been using to document all my proof.

I frantically looked for it everywhere. Retracing my steps, I went back to the Church History Library and

---

82 Bashore, Melvin L. "Behind Adobe Walls and Iron Bars: The Utah Territorial Penitentiary Library." Libraries & Culture 38, no. 3 (2003): 236-249. (https://doi.org/10.1353/lac.2003.0037 Accessed 15 June 2024).

asked them about their lost and found. Apparently, anything lost in and around Temple Square gets taken to the basement of the Conference Center. It was quite eerie down there. It started with a long, half-dark cement corridor and ended at a large cut-out with a metal desk manned by a security guard. No one had turned in a large black flash drive on a lanyard. I checked the Utah State Archives, but no luck there either. I had to redo a bunch of my research, but I was much more thorough the second time around in case I had missed something. I was also saving my research on several flash drives and my Google Drive so there wouldn't be another loss.

To triple-check my latest find, I searched for William and Charly Ross on the prisoner roster microfilm in my possession. That told me that Charly Ross was not my Charles F. Rose. The most obvious factor was that my Charles F. Rose was thirty years old in 1886 and Charly Ross was twenty-one years old in 1886. The math simply does not hold up.

16 Park City Museum Research Center

I took advantage of an opportunity to get off work early one day and headed back to the Park City Museum, I did not know that there was a research center in the basement on the other side of the building then the Dungeon was located the last time I was at the Museum.

"I heard that there is a research center in the basement. Is that true?" I asked the ladies at the front desk after I walked in.

"Yes."

"Is there a way for me to be able to gain access to the research center in the basement?"

"Do you have an appointment?"

"I need an appointment?! You only just confirmed for me that there was a research center in the basement. How would I have an appointment? I have come from Heber City, and I do not know when my next day off from work will be. I just happened to be able to get off work early today and came here to ask questions."

Shock and confusion filled their faces. One of them recovered faster than the other. "Let me call down there and see if they will let you go down," she said.

"Thank you."

Five minutes later, I was in the basement, opposite The Dungeon. The research center was about twenty feet from the elevator doors. It had double doors, like the ones you often see in older buildings. The metal frames included a small window in each door. When I walked in, there were four computers directly in front of me for patrons' use, a few filing cabinets, and bookshelves. There were a couple of wooden tables to the left, one of which was covered in papers as someone did their own research. The room was not very big, maybe about twenty feet by twenty feet. To my right was a door and some windows that you could look through. That next room was much larger and went a long way back. It had more bookshelves and filing cabinets.

I was greeted by a man. I can't remember his name,

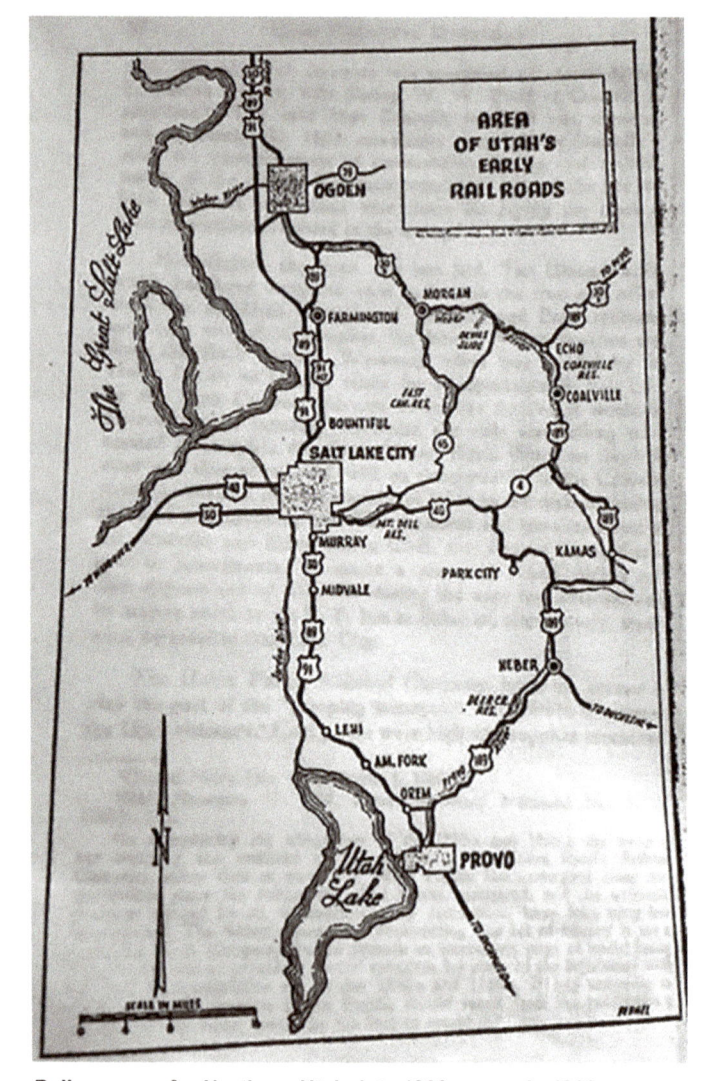

Railway map for Northern Utah, late 1800s or early 1900s

but he was in charge of the research center. He gave me a short tour, noting that the much larger room was the main archives and that only employees were allowed back there. The room that we stood in was the reading room, where patrons could do research and get one-on-one help. I thanked him for the tour and first asked questions about a couple of people with the last name of Rose I had found in one of Gary Kimball's books. No luck there.

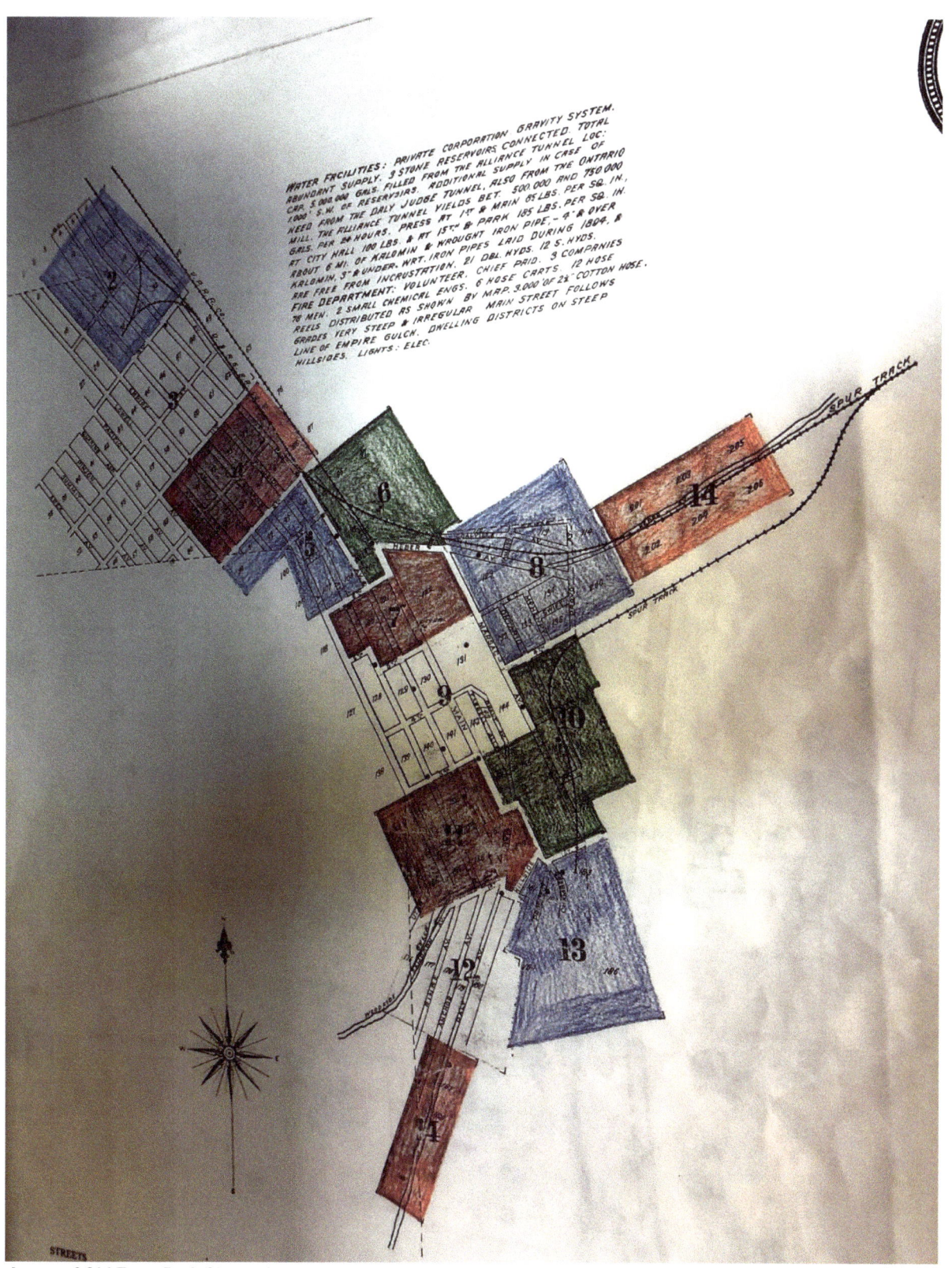

A map of Old Town Park City and the railway line in 1907

Next, I asked about where the railways used to be around Park City in the late 1800s and early 1900s.[83] It was by rail that all three of my ancestors were taken to the Utah Territorial Penitentiary to await trial. The director was more than happy to show me the original railroad plans for the area.[84]

The main train depot had only been down the road a couple of blocks on historical Main Street and Heber Avenue.

Utah's main railroad system used to be along the main highways and freeways, U.S. 40 and Highway 80. Many of the current walking and biking trails in and around Park City are where the railways once were. They are called the Rail Trails.

Today, there are three white buildings in historic downtown Park City that were once part of the train depot. One is an art gallery, one is a spa, and the last one is a restaurant called Courchevel Bistro.[85]

This restaurant is owned by the Talisker Club, a private ski and golf club with a gated community in the Park City area. The restaurant building was the main train station.

My third-great-grandfather and his daughter, my second-great-grandmother, were taken to the Utah Territorial Penitentiary by train from Old Town Park City to Sugar House in Salt Lake City. Finding out where the old train depot was and to stand where my ancestors stood was overwhelming and surreal. It was sobering, and I felt honored to retrace their footsteps in some way.

While I was at the research center, I also found a newspaper article about Charles F. Rose. This article stated that Charles was held in prison with a $500 bond in 1886 after his arrest.

That was a lot of money in the 1800s. In today's money, that would be $16,332.50.

---

83 Photo of a Map of Old Town Park City and the Railway Line in 1907, Map Kept in the Reacher Center in the Basement of The Park City Museum, (Photo taken by Jubilee Haddessa on 9 January 2020).

84 Photo of Railway Map for Northern Utah Late 1800s early 1900s, Map Kept in the Reacher Center in the Basement of The Park City Museum, (Photo taken by Jubilee Haddessa on 9 January 2020).

85 Photos of The Old Train Station as it looked in 2020, On Main Street and Heber Ave, in old town Park City (Photo taken by Jubilee Haddessa on 9 January 2020).

Unraveling the Family Secret

17 Cemetery, Nearly Lost To Time

I gained more than one lead at RootsTech 2020, the tenth anniversary of the largest genealogical conference in the world. The three-day conference of classes and networking, where I talked to the older woman about researching German relatives, was held at the Salt Palace in Salt Lake City. While I was waiting for my next class in a large ballroom outfitted with a portable stage, large projection screen, and about a hundred soft-cushioned chairs in neat rows, I overheard two ladies behind me discussing "virtual cemeteries." Intrigued, I apologized for my accidental eavesdropping and told them I had to know what they meant.

One of the ladies laughed. "Eavesdropping is how we get our best genealogical information," she said.

The other one explained they were talking about Findagrave.com and its app, where people can volunteer to go to a cemetery and take photos of the headstones to upload to the Findagrave.com database. This helps millions of people find where their ancestors were buried. The app is amazing. It showed me several smaller cemeteries in Wasatch County that I had not known existed before. My thoughts were maybe I could find where Charles F. Rose was buried this way.

The first cemetery to be dedicated in Heber Valley was up Center Creek. It was a small pioneer cemetery. The Find a Grave app led me to a historical monument put up by the Daughters of the Utah Pioneers in 1956 at a Church of Jesus Christ of Latter-day Saints Chapel on South Mill Road and Center Creek Road.

This monument's message led me to drive up Center Creek Road.[86] On the left of the road about a mile from the first monument was a large sandstone rock that stated that the Pioneer Cemetery was somewhere up ahead, along with some GPS coordinates. This stone was placed in front of an old beautiful red brick building that I am pretty sure was an early chapel of the Church of the Jesus Christ of Latter-day Saints. It might be a preschool now.[87]

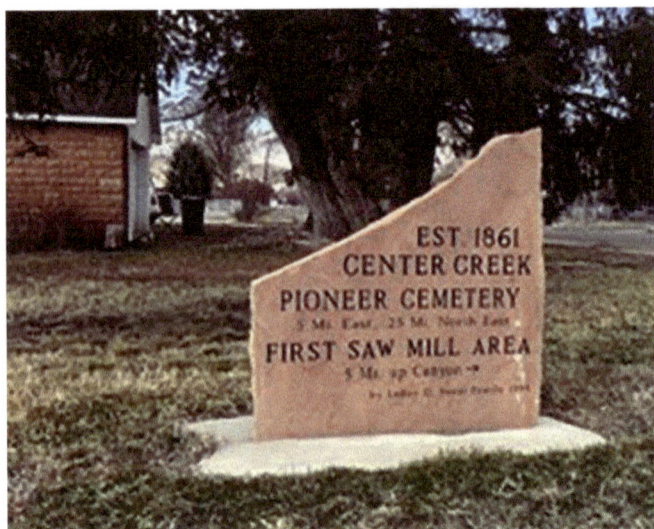

---

[86] Photo of Daughters of the Utah Pioneers Monument #226, Heber City, Utah (Photo taken by Jubilee Haddessa on 10 March 2020).

[87] Photo of Sandstone Monument in Center Creek, Heber City, Utah (Photo taken by Jubilee Haddessa on 10 March 2020).

After inputting the coordinates into my phone, I drove to where my app told me to go. A couple of miles later, there were only houses and empty fields. The coordinates were telling me that the cemetery could be in someone's backyard.

It was time to start knocking on doors. Later, when I was telling my mother about how I found it, she was surprised that I would just start knocking on doors.

"Mom, how else was I going to find it?" I asked her. "I figured that the locals in the community would know where it was. If you have questions, you need to ask real people for the answers."

My mom sighed at that and walked away. She never wants to be a burden to other people. However, if a person does not talk to other people and ask questions, nothing would ever get done.

The first door that I knocked on was answered by a nice gentleman.

"Hello! This is going to sound odd," I told him, "but I am looking for a cemetery that the coordinates brought me to your house, but I do not see any headstones nearby. You wouldn't know anything about it, would you?"

He was happy to tell me all about the Pioneer Cemetery. We walked through his house and onto his back deck. He pointed to a flagpole with Old Glory flying proudly, up on a hill in the distance in the middle of the field behind his house and past two wire fences.[88] "See where that flagpole is? That's where the cemetery you are looking for is. My great-grandfather is buried there."

"How many people are buried there?"

"I don't know. Probably about fifty, maybe more."

He explained that they used to put cemeteries two stone throws from the road. Who threw the stone would determine how far from the road a cemetery would be created. This cemetery was the first in the Heber area. Center Creek happened to be the first settlement in Heber Valley because of all the timber that had been there. That is why the area was called Old Mill.

The developer who bought the field a few years back attempted to dig it up to start construction. That riled up all the neighbors in the area. They went out to meet the person who was operating the backhoe with shotguns to protect the cemetery. They did not want

Angel wings on the fence of a cemetery mean that some of the people buried there died quite young. They are with the angels now, safe and sound.

the backhoe driver destroying the graves. This show of force shut down the whole operation, even to this day. After that, there was a fence put up around the cemetery, and the flagpole was erected in the middle of it to honor those who were buried there.

---

88 Photos of Old Pioneer Cemetery in Center Creek, Heber City, Utah (Photo taken by Jubilee Haddessa on 10 March 2020).

The gentlemen told me that a couple of other people had asked about the cemetery in recent years as well. I was given permission to jump his fences to go explore the cemetery. He said the locals would know why I was out in the field and wouldn't bat an eye, even though there was a *NO TRESPASSERS* sign on the main gate. He suggested clearing up and maintaining the cemetery would be a great Eagle Scout project. He gave me his phone number, just in case I had any questions about the cemetery in the future.

Jumping two fences was not my idea of fun, even though I had done it before. I went looking for an easier way to get there. I knocked on one more door down the hill a little bit from the gentlemen's home. A lady answered the door. We conversed about the cemetery.

"Is there an easier way to get there, besides climbing several fences?"

"I would let you go through my horse corrals, but they are all full of freezing mud right now," she said. "I don't think you want to crawl through the mud, but go for it if that is what you want to do."

I thanked her and again started looking for an easier way after she closed the door. There was a determination in my bones to get to that cemetery. It was going to happen somehow, some way that very day, even if I had to trudge through freezing mud or jump fences. This was a forgotten cemetery, and the people buried there deserved better. Heck, maybe Charles F. Rose was buried there, and he was trying to tell me that from beyond the grave.

After a few more minutes of searching for a better way to get to the cemetery, I found a gap at the corner of two intersecting fences. One was a wire fence attached to a large wood pole, and the other was a white picket fence. There was about a one-foot gap between the two, and I shimmied through it sideways. From there, it was just a matter of walking up the sagebrush-covered hill to the cemetery. It was only about a ten-minute walk from the main road, where I had parked my car on the shoulder in the grass.

When I arrived at the cemetery, I was so overwhelmed with emotion that I bawled my eyes out. I am unsure why I cried. All I knew was everyone who was buried there was happy that I had found them. They were happy that someone, anyone, was making an effort to know them and to remember them. I am pretty sure there were more than fifty people buried there, but it was hard to tell.

There were so many red sandstone headstones that were blank, and some were broken.

Some even said, *KNOWN ONLY TO GOD*.

There were two large red sandstone headstones broken and lying on the ground in what looked like cement. Someone had tried to fix them on the ground. The names and dates were hard to read because the "fixed" pieces were not entirely aligned; none of the broken edges were touching. Some of the pieces were flipped to the wrong side, obscuring some of the writing. I imagined trying to piece the gravestone back together in a field with only wet cement that the person had to haul out there themselves—probably with a wheelbarrow, a shovel, and maybe a trowel of some sort—must have been almost impossible. I am grateful for whoever attempted to piece these two headstones back together. Thank you to whoever did the cement work.

There was also a Daughters of the Utah Pioneers historical monument that had nine names on it.[89] This monument matched the one down at the church house of the Church of Jesus Christ of Latter-day Saints on Mill Road and Center Street:

- Luttie Cluff
- Eliza Foster Cluff
- Hammond, a Hawaiian
- William Cole
- Rebecca R. Cole
- Samuel McRae Rooker
- Emily W. Rooker
- Jens N. Miller (One of the broken-up red sandstone headstones is his.)
- Anna M. Miller (The other broken-up red sandstone headstone is hers.)

Many hours were spent at this cemetery in meditation, pondering, and just feeling safe on sacred ground. My mother, my sister and her family, and one of my good friends have all humored me by taking the small hike up there to explore the cemetery with me on separate occasions. They all felt honored that I would show them this sacred place.

In March 2020, this started a new journey from the one that originally had the goal of finding out where Charles F. Rose was buried.

Exploring cemeteries all but lost to time has been very special for me.

---

89 Photos of Old Pioneer Cemetery in Center Creek, Heber City, Utah (Photo taken by Jubilee Haddessa on 10 March 2020).

Jubilee Haddessa

18 Details Matter

In April 2020, I was looking over the early church records of the membership of Peter Tonge's family in the Church of Jesus Christ of Latter-day Saints for a second time more closely.[90] A gut feeling told me I had missed something. Rule One of research: Always read the document more than once, and try to do so a few months apart.

Something had caught my eye. One document had two Nancy Tonges.

One Nancy Tonge was born in Farnworth, Bolton, England, on March 2, 1869, and died in 1870. The other Nancy Ellen Tonge was born in Farnworth, Bolton, England, on January 8, 1871, or 1872. They were born only a few years apart.

I could not believe that I had found another person, another baby lost in time. Sometimes, a person is only ever mentioned on one document, and then they are gone. If a researcher was lucky, that person had a name and a birth date written down. Other times, the person was only mentioned in a general way—baby, child, boy, girl, woman, man, wife, or husband—with no name or dates given. Those are depressing to come across.

I have no idea how I missed the first Nancy Tonge on this document. She was only a baby when she passed away. Nancy makes five people that were somehow overlooked when people were first researching this family line.

---

90 "The Church of Jesus Christ of Latter-Day Saints Membership records, U.S.A. and Canada; Heber East Ward Records of Members Early 1902" images, Family History Library, (FHL, Salt Lake City, Utah: Accessed 11 May 2019), Church records of the Tonges, Libr. No. 13271, Microfilm Number 0026026, About Page 51.

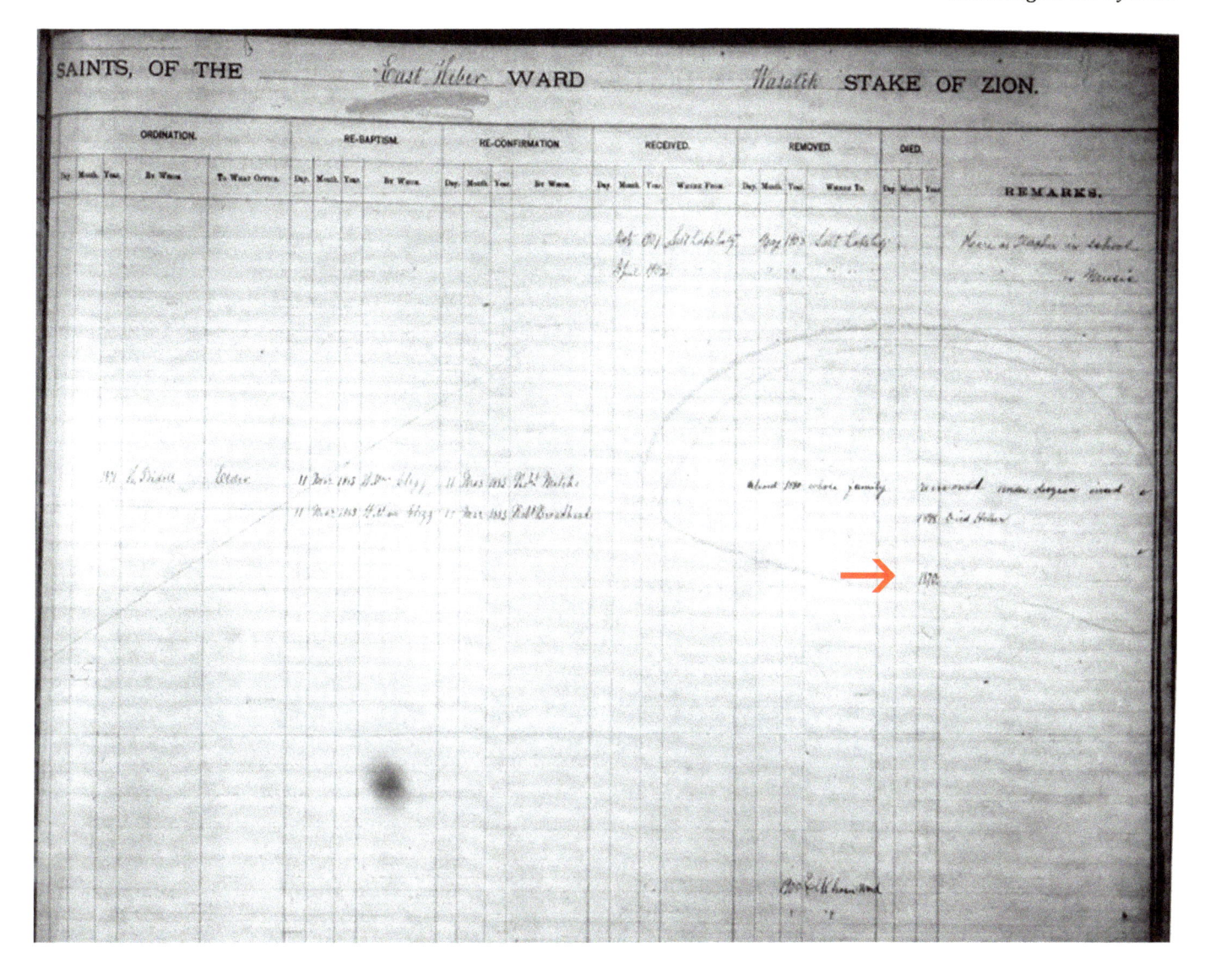

- Two baby daughters of Peter and Elizabeth Tonge, Nancy and Mary E.
- Two babies of Sarah Tonge, no name or gender given
- Last but not least, my biological second-great-grandfather, Charles F. Rose

As I am writing this, I am absolutely positive there are many more people nearly lost to time, waiting to be rediscovered.

At its core, family history is all about connecting people to the right people, learning about them and their lives, and not letting anyone become forgotten. In return, our ancestors' stories can and will sustain us and help us navigate through our own challenges.

In June 2020, I was doing some more research on my great-grandmother Maude Alice Sabey Thompson's children. On the birth certificate for Alice Thompson—Maude's eldest daughter—it stated that Maude was born in Alma, Wyoming . . . not Evanston, like I was always told.[91]

---

[91] Wallsburg, Wasatch, Utah, USA, "Utah State Archives Indexes," database with images, Utah State Archives, (https://ww.archives.utah.gov/indexes: accessed 13 March 2021), Birth Certificate of Alice Thompson, (b. 1909); Department of Health. Office of Vital Records and Statistics, Series 81448, File #: 75.

Almy, Wyoming
Ghost town

Location within the state of Wyoming
○ Show map of Wyoming
○ Show map of the United States
○ Show all

Coordinates: 41°33′17″N 111°00′39″W

Country	United States
State	Wyoming
County	Uinta

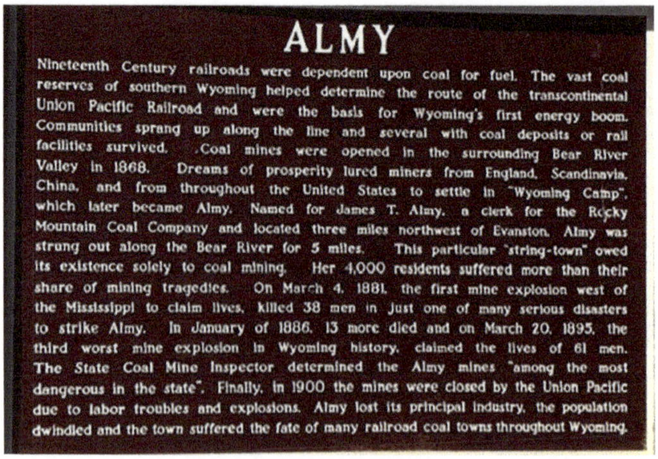

ALMY
Nineteenth Century railroads were dependent upon coal for fuel. The vast coal reserves of southern Wyoming helped determine the route of the transcontinental Union Pacific Railroad and were the basis for Wyoming's first energy boom. Communities sprang up along the line and several with coal deposits or rail facilities survived. Coal mines were opened in the surrounding Bear River Valley in 1868. Dreams of prosperity lured miners from England, Scandinavia, China, and from throughout the United States to settle in "Wyoming Camp", which later became Almy. Named for James T. Almy, a clerk for the Rocky Mountain Coal Company and located three miles northwest of Evanston, Almy was strung out along the Bear River for 5 miles. This particular "string-town" owed its existence solely to coal mining. Her 4,000 residents suffered more than their share of mining tragedies. On March 4, 1881, the first mine explosion west of the Mississippi to claim lives, killed 38 men in just one of many serious disasters to strike Almy. In January of 1886, 13 more died and on March 20, 1895, the third worst mine explosion in Wyoming history, claimed the lives of 61 men. The State Coal Mine Inspector determined the Almy mines "among the most dangerous in the state". Finally, in 1900 the mines were closed by the Union Pacific due to labor troubles and explosions. Almy lost its principal industry, the population dwindled and the town suffered the fate of many railroad coal towns throughout Wyoming.

Google is your friend in any type of research project. By googling Alma, I found out that it never existed. However, there was a stringtown for coal miners called Almy, Wyoming, only a few miles outside of Evanston.[92] A stringtown is a line of homes or businesses situated along a railroad track.

My mother and I took a day trip to Almy, which was only about an hour's drive. This was a tiny town, probably about the size of Casper, Utah. If you blink, you have already driven though the whole town. I know now why everyone said that Sarah and Charles's daughter was born in Evanston instead of Almy. In the 1800s, people would name the larger town instead of a small spot out in the wilderness.

We found this historical marker about Almy on the side of the highway.[93]

---

92 Wikipedia, "Map of Almy, Wyoming", (Screen shot taken by Jubliee Haddessa on 24 June 2020).

93 Photo of Historical Marker about Almy on the Side of the Highway, Almy, Wyoming (Photo taken by Jubilee Haddessa on 24 June 2020).

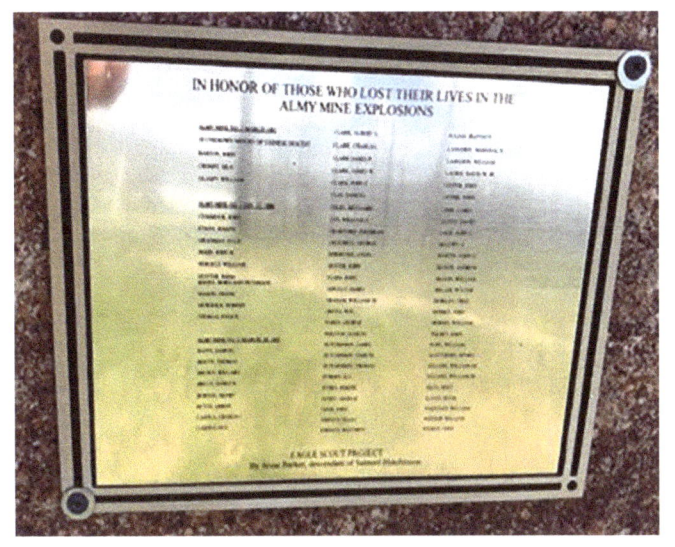

After driving around what was left of Almy, we found a sign that said *CEMETERY* and had an arrow on it pointing to the left.[94]

The best place to start research on a small, basically ghost town will always be the cemetery or cemeteries that lie within them.

One U-turn and about two miles later, we found the small Almy Cemetery.

None of the names of the headstones or in the record book there were any of my ancestors but it was still a place where one of my ancestors lived for a while. I loved exploring Almy, Wyoming.

---

94 Photos of Almy Cemetery 1881-1977, Almy, Wyoming (Photo taken by Jubilee Haddessa on 24 June 2020).

19 Insights On Peter Tonge

Deep in my heart and soul, I know that Peter Tonge never abused Sarah in any way. He was the only one who was on her side and the only one trying to protect his daughter when everyone else turned their backs.

Peter was even a witness to Sarah's marriage to James Sabey on October 1, 1897, in Wallsburg, Utah, in the home of James Sabey.[95]

---

[95] "Utah, Marriages 1887-1940," images, FamilySearch, (http://www.familysearch.org: accessed 4 April 2020,) Marriage License of James Sabey and Sarah Tonge, (1 October 1897), Microfilm#: 004579394, page 200, photocopy in the possession of the preparer (2020).

Peter was also in Sarah Sabey's household on the 1920 federal census in Provo, Utah, with a few of her younger children.⁹⁶

If he was guilty of constantly raping his daughter, why was he in her home near her children?

If Sarah was anything like me, I would never have allowed Peter anywhere near my children if he had ever abused me in any way.

I would have killed him before he could have touched any of my children.

---

96 Familysearch, "1920 U.S. Census," database with images, FamilySearch (https://www.familysearch.org: accessed 1 January 2021), Peter Tonge in household of Sarah Sabey, Utah, Utah, United States; citing, sheet, line, family, NARA microfilm publication T625 (Washington D.C.: National Archives and Records Administration, 1992), roll ; FHL microfilm

Jubilee Haddessa

20 More Investigation On the Spratleys

A friend of mine contacted me via text about an estate sale in American Fork, Utah. She had found an advertisement on Facebook, but the kicker was a sign out front. The house's lamp post held a plaque that stated SPRATLEY HOUSE, EST. 1872.[97]

"Isn't Spratley a surname you are researching?" she asked me.

"Yes! Thank you so much for sharing this information with me."

I am so blessed that my friends who know about my journey will share leads they come across by just living their lives. It was surprising that there was a house that still existed in American Fork that the Spratleys had owned once upon a time.

My mom, my niece, and I went to investigate this house in person. The ad said that the estate sale was a block south of the American Fork Library. That is all the directions I really had. We went around in circles for a bit until we finally found it.[98]

We looked around the outside of the home. I felt humbled walking where people I was actively researching had walked. Was this the home of Jedediah Spratley? I do not know. What I do know is there were many Spratleys who lived in American Fork in the late 1800s. They were all related in one way or another. I am sure that Jedediah Spratley at least visited that home.

It was a rather large home for a building that was built in the late 1800s. There must have been some additions to it over the years. It was beautiful. We could not go inside because it was for sale. We walked around the front and took some pictures. We didn't dare try to walk around to the back for fear that someone might call the local police on us, thinking we were trespassing or casing the place to rob later.

---

97 Photo of Facebook Ad of an Estate Sale for a House in American Fork, Utah that had a Sign Out Front that said, "Spratley House EST. 1872", (Screen Shot taken by (private) a friend of Jubilee Haddessa on 18 July 2020).

98 Photos of the Spratley House EST. 1872 in American Fork, Utah, (Photos taken by Jubilee Haddessa on 18 July 2020).

Unraveling the Family Secret

About a year later, I was compelled to go find Jedediah's headstone in the American Fork Cemetery. I jumped in my car on July 31, 2021, and made the drive there from my home.

The first step on arriving at the cemetery was to find the plot map and look for the Spratleys.[99] I was surprised that there were only nine Spratleys in the cemetery. Back in 2019, I had found far more than nine church records of the Church of Jesus Christ of Latter-Day Saints for the surname Spratley in the Family History Library in Salt Lake City.

It was a very hot summer day, and it took about two hours of walking around the cemetery and a short, heartfelt prayer before I finally found his headstone.[100] The cemetery plot map was not as easily followed as the one in the Provo Pioneer Cemetery.

I spent a few minutes in silence pondering what I knew about Jedidiah Spratley, which wasn't a lot. He married a different woman, Nettie Mann, sometime after he and Sarah Tonge had their affair. Then, he and his wife got a divorce sometime later. They did not have any children. There is also not much known about Nettie, just that she was married to him for a bit.

I just knew he was there, and I told him I had no hard feelings toward him. There was no judgment from me about his past actions whatsoever, since we are all human and make mistakes. We need to be given a little grace from our fellow humans and so much grace from ourselves.

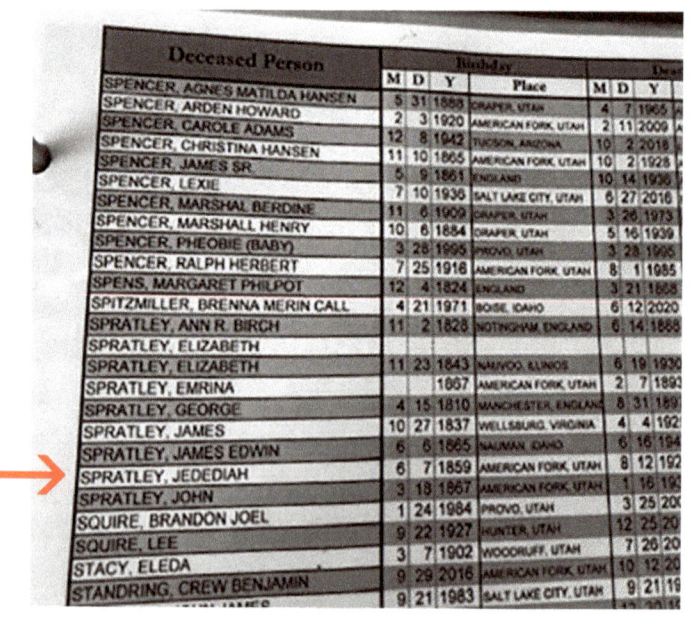

American Fork Cemetery plot map

Jedidiah Spratley's headstone

---

99 Photo of Cemetery Records in American Fork, Utah Cemetery, (Photos taken by Jubilee Haddessa on 31 July 2021).

100 Photo of Jedidiah Spratley's Headstone in American Fork, Utah Cemetery, (Photos taken by Jubilee Haddessa on 31 July 2021).

21 Insights On James Sabey

James Sabey had been married twice before he met and married my second-great-grandmother, Sarah Tonge. He had several children from his previous wives, and he was a widower. Sarah was living in American Fork, Utah, when they first met. She answered an ad that James had put out, seeking help running a home. Sarah began working as a domestic servant in James's household in America Fork.

According to original family group sheets passed down from my parents to me, Sarah and James had a daughter named Elizabeth.[101] She was buried in the Wallsburg Cemetery. Her headstone just reads Lizzie.[102] It is odd that there are no dates on the headstone, but it might mean that she was a baby when she passed. She was obviously important to James Sabey—important enough to bury her in his own plot.

On the family group sheets, Lizzie was born October 4, 1897, in Wallsburg, Utah, and died January 27, 1898. James Sabey and Sarah Tonge were married on October 1, 1897.[103] This would mean that James and Sarah had gotten pregnant out of wedlock or that Lizzie was not James's biological daughter. Either way, I am forever grateful that James decided to marry Sarah. He could have just turned his back on all of them when she was heavily pregnant and was caring for her three other children. He took them all in and treated them as his very own in a time and place where unwed mothers were very much scorned.

He became a father to three children that he did not

Elizabeth "Lizzie" Sabey's headstone

have any responsibility or relation to. He married and loved a woman with a very checkered past and did not care what the world had to say about it, as evidenced by the fact they went on to have several more children. To me, he was a hero and the best example of a man and father.

James's side of the family and his older children did not like Sarah at all. They mostly shunned her and their own father after James and Sarah got married. The couple moved from American Fork to just outside Wallsburg Valley in Provo Canyon and started a homestead near where Main Creek empties out into the Provo River (See Chapter 12).[104]

---

101 Original Sabey Family Group Sheets, (In the possession of Jubilee Haddessa, 8 August 2024).

102 Photo of Elizabeth Sabey's Headstone, Wallsburg Cemetery, Wallsburg, Utah, (Photo taken by Jubilee Haddessa on 27 May 2019).

103 "Utah, Marriages 1887-1940," images, FamilySearch, (http://www.familysearch.org: accessed 4 April 2020,) Marriage License of James Sabey and Sarah Tonge, (1 October 1897), Microfilm#: 004579394, page 200, photocopy in the possession of the preparer (2020).

104 Wasatch County, Utah, USA, "The Homestead Patent of James Sabey and Sarah Tonge," Wasatch County Recorder's Office, Heber City, Wasatch, Utah, USA. (Accessed: 23 Jun 2019) Photocopies in the position of the preparer. From Book P. Certificate number: 44908.

There are two identical headstones for James Sabey in his cemetery plot in the Wallsburg Cemetery, Wallsburg, Utah.[105] One is about two feet farther west than the other one. Apparently, one side of the Sabey family says that he is buried in one spot and the other side of the family says he is buried in the other spot. So, two different headstones were placed to stop the hurtful words and to stop a family feud in its tracks. This was an expensive compromise; a small flat headstone runs for about $1,500, maybe more, in today's money.

My dad made sure that I knew our side of the family thinks James Sabey is buried closer to the east. This goes to show how petty humans can be toward each other. It is sad, really. It does not matter in the long run which burial site holds James. Everyone knows he is buried in the Wallsburg Cemetery.

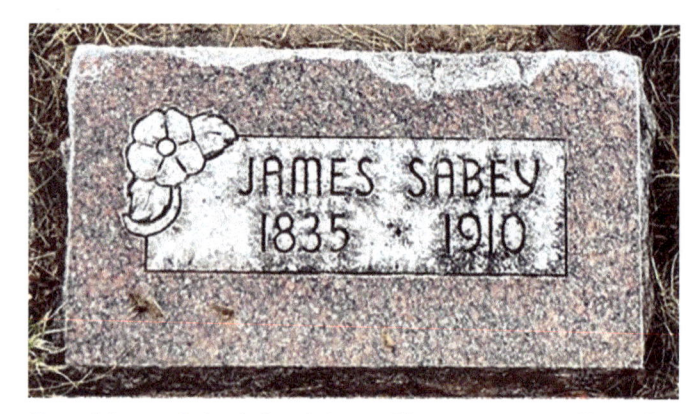

One of James Sabey's headstones. They are exact replicas of each other only four feet apart

I just don't understand why or how humans can be so mean to one another. Maybe I never will. This is just another example of how at odds this family really is—and has been.

---

105 Photo of James Sabey's Headstone in Wallsburg Cemetery, Wallsburg, Utah, (Photo taken by Jubilee Haddessa on 27 May 2019).

Epilogue

Although this journey is not over, this research and all the people involved in it have sustained me through some very dark places in my life. I feel like, even though most of these people lived over 120 years ago and most died more than fifty years ago, that they are very close friends of mine. Living people are harder for me to connect with than the dead. The more I learn about the Tonges, James Sabey, and Charles F. Rose, the more I want to know. I feel like I could have actual conversations with any one of them and not be judged.

My passion for family history has turned into a lifelong quest. I hope that this story will touch people's souls as it did mine. We must accept the facts of history—the good, the bad, and the ugly. Learn from the facts and avoid repeating the mistakes; that is what history is for, not to be erased or hidden.

How else are we to become a better society together? Otherwise, we will be doomed to repeat the mistakes of those who have come before us.

Pedigree chart of my father's side

Some people have chosen to remain anonymous.

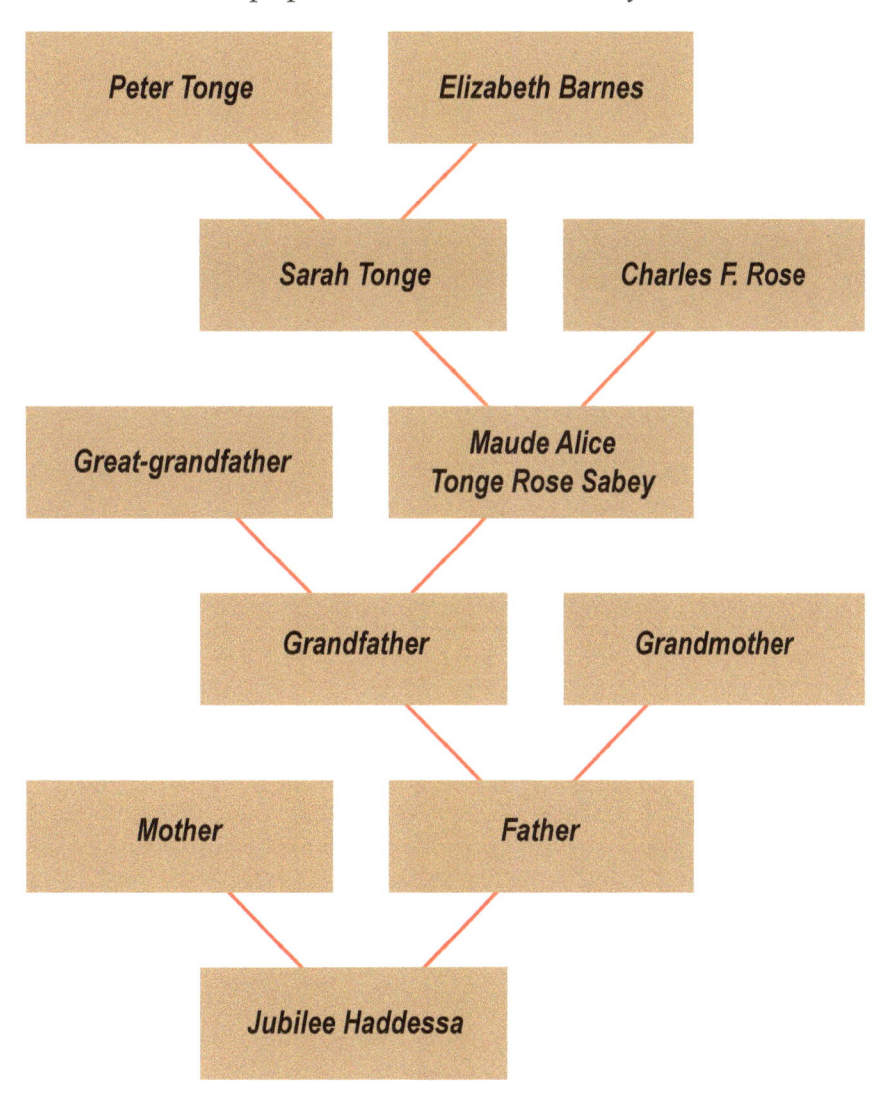

```
Peter Tonge      Elizabeth Barnes
        \       /
        Sarah Tonge          Charles F. Rose
                  \         /
Great-grandfather   Maude Alice
                    Tonge Rose Sabey
                \   /
              Grandfather        Grandmother
                       \         /
                   Mother    Father
                         \   /
                    Jubilee Haddessa
```

About the Author

Jubilee Haddessa was born and raised in Utah. She has two brothers and one sister, plus two nieces and five nephews. Mountains are ingrained in her very soul. She comes from hardy Utah pioneer stock. The stories of her ancestors are what sustain her daily. These stories have also raised questions about said ancestors that have sent her on a lifelong quest to find out all she can about the people who have come before. She believes every person has a story to share and that every person who ever lived or will live matters. No one is expendable. We all matter to someone, and those connections matter.

Jubilee owns her own family history research business. She wants to help anyone she can find the stories of their ancestors. She also sews, reads, and is an amateur photographer. She loves spending time with her dog.

Milton Keynes UK
Ingram Content Group UK Ltd.
UKHW052224171124
451301UK00005B/76